DATE DUE

ENGLISH CUSTOM
AND USAGE

1   The Dairymaids' May-day in London, *circa* 1750

Detail of a Painting by F. Hayman, engraved by C. Grignion
in a series executed for Vauxhall Gardens

ENGLISH CUSTOM & USAGE

By

CHRISTINA HOLE

ILLUSTRATED FROM
PRINTS AND PHOTOGRAPHS

LONDON
B. T. BATSFORD LTD.
15, North Audley Street, W.1

Republished by Omnigraphics ● Penobscot Building ● Detroit ● 1990

Works by the same Author:
TRADITIONS AND CUSTOMS
OF CHESHIRE
ENGLISH FOLKLORE
HAUNTED ENGLAND

First Published Winter 1941–2

Library of Congress Cataloging-in-Publication Data

Hole, Christina.
    English custom & usage / by Christina Hole.
        p.   cm.
    Reprint. Originally published: London : B.T. Batsford, 1941–1942.
    Includes bibliographical references.
    ISBN 1-55888-851-9 (lib. bdg. : alk. paper)
        1. Folklore—England.   2. England—Social life and customs.
    I. Title.   II. Title: English custom and usage.
    GR141.H593   1990
    398'.0942—dc20   89-63108
                                                                      CIP

Printed in the United States of America.

PREFACE

IN this book I have attempted to give a brief description of some of the traditional customs and ceremonies which still exist in England, together with a short account of their origin and history. Considerations of space make it impossible to describe every ancient survival or revival which can still be seen in different parts of the country. Their number is a refreshing proof of the tenacity of tradition and the love of the English for the old and beautiful customs of their ancestors. A few of these ceremonies have had to be suspended during the present war, particularly those which involve bonfires and illuminations, or large nocturnal gatherings, but I am assured by the people of most districts concerned that this interruption is only temporary. Many of the customs here described have continued for centuries; others have been revived after a lapse of time. Sometimes they exist only in a corrupted or mutilated form, and in too many cases their real meaning has been almost lost sight of, and their existence is locally explained by some more recent legend which veils their true antiquity. All have been described before, and from the very nature of the subject there can be little new to offer to the reader. But these customs are a part of our national heritage, and it is well worth our while to make some effort to understand and preserve them. Their disappearance would be an irreparable loss to the folk-lorist and the antiquarian, and even more so, perhaps, to all who love colour, diversity and individualism, and dread the monotonous uniformity which seems to be one of the insidious diseases of modern life.

I have been privileged to see many of these ceremonies myself, and others have been carefully described to me by competent eyewitnesses. I have to record my most grateful thanks to the many correspondents, and particularly to the Rectors and Vicars of many parishes, who have taken infinite trouble and given much of their valuable time to inform me of the details, past and present, of ceremonies in their districts, who have allowed me to read old books and documents in their possession, who have told me of local traditions, and who have made it possible for me in a number of cases to be present at the ceremonies themselves. Without such generous help as I have received, I could not have hoped to complete this brief account, and to all who have assisted me in these ways and given me the benefit of their own knowledge, I offer my very sincere thanks.

CHRISTINA HOLE

OXFORD,
Summer 1941

ACKNOWLEDGMENT

ONCE again the Publishers have to thank Messrs. W. T. Spencer for putting at the book's disposal their vast and unique collection of social prints, which Miss Watkins has handled with marked ability; Figs. 4, 14, 15, 24, 25, 32–35, 52, 61 and the frontispiece áre from this source. The provenance of the photographs is as follows: Messrs. G. P. Abraham, Ltd., 58; Mr. E. W. Attwood, Oxford, 72; the *Berwick Journal*, 12; the City of Birmingham Reference Library, 45, 74 (the latter from the Sir Benjamin Stone Collection of Photographs in their possession); The Central Press, Ltd., 5, 16, 48, 66, 70, 76, 91; Exclusive News Agency Ltd., 68; the *Folklore Calendar*, by George Long (Philip Allan & Co., 1930), 19–21, the photographs by the author; Fox Photos, Ltd., 2, 3, 6, 17, 18, 22, 23, 27, 29, 31, 38, 39, 42–4, 55, 56, 59, 63, 64, 68, 69, 71, 73, 78, 81, 84, 88; the *Illustrated London News*, 3 6; the *Leicester Evening Mail*, 40, 41; Messrs. Dorien Leigh, Ltd., 50, 82, 83; the Oxford Public Library (by the late H. W. Taunt), 46; the *Oxford Times and Mail*, 13, 49, 51, 67; Messrs. Walter Scott, Bradford, 79; *The Times*, 28, 37, 60, 65, 77, 80, 85; Miss M. Wight, p. 85 (drawn by Miss E. Alldridge); Mr. F. R. Winstone, Bristol, 54, 57, 86, 87, 89, 90; Mr. G. Bernard Wood, Leeds, 9, 10, 53.

CONTENTS

2 The Clipping Ceremony, Painswick Churchyard

3 The Horn Dance, Abbot's Bromley, Staffordshire

4 Gathering and putting on May-day green boughs and garlands

From an eighteenth-century engraving

Chapter I

PAGAN SURVIVALS

IT is very usually said that old customs and ceremonies are fast dying out everywhere, and that in this modern and mechanical age there is no room for those curious survivals which once formed a direct link with the past, often with a very remote past indeed. This is a statement which commands attention if only because it has been repeated so often and for so long. In the eighteenth century writers lamented or rejoiced, according to temperament, at the decline of traditional rites and prophesied their imminent total extinction, and the polite and ultra-reasonable gentry of that period did their best to make the prophecy come true by abolishing many a rural feast because it led to rowdiness, and converting mediaeval doles to more utilitarian purposes, or doing away with them altogether. Victorian observers wrote patronisingly of old customs as rude survivals from a less enlightened age which the new knowledge of science and mechanics would certainly sweep away within a few years. In our own time, the motor-bus, the cinematograph, and the wireless are cited as reasons for the weakening of rural community life and the consequent destruction of the communal rejoicings and ceremonies which once formed so important a part of the year's round. In all this there is a great deal of truth. New and easier forms of amusement have replaced the old games and dances, modern economic conditions have largely destroyed the agricultural and trade festivities, and a greater degree of self-consciousness has made the simple and often rough pleasures of our ancestors difficult for us. Nevertheless, a host of traditional customs still survive in many districts in their full vigour, and others have been revived of late years. Many indeed have died out beyond hope of resurrection and others exist only in a fragmentary or mutilated form. Yet here and there, in city and village alike, the old spirit rears its head in due season, and ancient rites are carried on at the same time and in the same place as they were centuries ago.

Such survivals and revivals deserve some study. Too often

I

their true origin and meaning are overlooked; those who take part in them do so because it is the custom, and the spectator sees only something quaint and charming, worth preserving, perhaps, because of its intrinsic beauty and traditional association with a particular locality, but otherwise devoid of interest. Sometimes the great age of a local custom is veiled by an explanatory legend which has been invented after the real origin has been completely forgotten. Because of this lack of understanding, an interruption of a few years, such as a war or other upheaval may cause, is often enough to destroy the practice of centuries because, continuity having once been broken, there seems to be no particular reason for beginning again. Yet if all such customs were swept away or allowed to die out, the country would be immeasurably the poorer for their loss. Nearly all can teach us something about forgotten ways of life and work. Many spring from the ancient and primitive rites by which our remoter ancestors strove to influence nature and the fertility of crops, while others commemorate some historical event which once influenced men's lives for good or evil. It may be worth while, therefore, to set on record some of the customs which still survive in this country, and to try and trace their source and meaning before it is too late.

Many of our older traditional customs are pagan in origin and carry us back to a very remote period in our history. The human mind is very tenacious of old habits and loyalties, especially where religion is concerned, and the wholesale conversions of early times did not always sink very deep. Though many undoubtedly embraced Christianity from real spiritual conviction, there were others, and perhaps the majority, who remained pagan in their hearts and adopted the new religion only on the orders of their lord or chief, or from some hope of worldly advantage. Many did not clearly understand the strange doctrine, and a man might well be a baptised Christian and yet retain some secret leanings towards the discarded gods of his fathers. The wiser missionaries realised the great power of old association and these, where they failed to uproot, often tried to adapt and modify well-established and loved customs. In A.D. 601 Pope Gregory wrote to Abbot Mellitus, saying he had given much thought to "the affair of the English," and considered that pagan temples should not be destroyed, but rather be purified with holy water, the idols within them abolished, and Christian altars set up in their place. In these familiar, if slightly altered, surroundings, the people could be won more easily to the new faith. And he goes on:

". . . because they have been accustomed to slaughter many oxen to devils, some solemnity must be exchanged for them on this account, so that on the day of the dedication, or the nativities of the holy martyrs, whose relics are there deposited, they may build themselves huts of the boughs of trees about those churches which have been turned to that use from temples, and celebrate the solemnity with religious feasting, and no more offer beasts to the devil, but kill cattle to the praise of God in their eating, and return thanks to the giver of all things for their sustenance."

The wise and human policy outlined in this letter turned many pagan festivals into Christian feast-days. November 1st was a day of worship before it became All Saints' Day, and the Winter Solstice was observed with rejoicing and sacrifice before there were any Christians in England to keep Christmas Day. The wells whose spirits had formerly been adored were re-dedicated to saints to whose intercession the cures performed at healing wells were ascribed. The transformed temples were replaced in the course of time by new and permanent churches, and it is interesting to note that there are some sites in this country where worship, pagan or Christian, has been carried on in unbroken succession for many centuries.

It is perhaps unnecessary to say that matters were not always so easily arranged. For many years after England was professedly Christian, the old gods still held secret sway, especially in times of trouble. The Church had to wage continuous warfare against the forces of reaction. In an age when paganism flourished openly in some European countries and had not long been overcome in others, constant watchfulness was necessary, and the more ardent and fanatical priests sometimes came into violent collision with the silent and obstinate conservatism of the people. The defeated gods were not thought of as simple illusions, even by their enemies; the latter regarded them as living and active devils who strove constantly to destroy Christian souls. Many ancient customs connected with the soil, the harvest, and the fertility of women or cattle stank in the nostrils of the clergy as wiles of the Evil One. Nor were

3

they always wrong in supposing that such rites remained as heathen as ever, in spite of the alleged Christianity of those who took part in them. Even after some five hundred years had passed since England's conversion, Canute found it necessary in 1018 to enact laws against the worship of the sun and moon and of trees, wells and stones. The observance of the Calends of January, when men dressed themselves in the skins and heads of animals and ran leaping and prancing through the streets, was forbidden again and again, but apparently with little or no effect. In the seventh century, Theodore, Archbishop of Canterbury, ordered "for those who in such wise transform themselves into the appearance of a wild animal, penance for three years because this is devilish." The practice seems to have been already ancient in his day and probably originated in prehistoric times. A Palaeolithic drawing on the walls of the Caverne des Trois Frères at Ariège shows a man dressed in a stag's skin and wearing antlers on his head, and a bone engraving of the same period which was found in Pinhole Cave, Derbyshire, depicts a man whose face is masked by a horse's head. An altar found under the Cathedral of Notre Dame in Paris and now in Cluny Museum shows the horned but human head of a Gaulish god to whom the Romans gave the name Cernunnos. It is probable that the animal-men of the Calends of January were connected with that horned god who, under different names, had been worshipped in Europe since the dawn of our history and, therefore, according to the ideas of his time, Theodore was quite correct in describing the custom as "devilish."

But in spite of these early struggles and difficulties, it is to the Church that we owe the preservation of some of our oldest and loveliest customs, as well as the institution of others almost equally interesting. When we come to discuss the seasonal customs of England we shall see how the old ideas that centred round the home and the growing of crops were transformed and Christianised, and how ancient rites in a new dress became part of the Christian religious life, as they had once been of heathen religious life. In our own day it has often been the parish clergy who have revived a local custom which had lapsed through indifference or been abolished because in the eighteenth or nineteenth centuries it had degenerated into little more than an opportunity for drinking and horseplay. So completely in many cases have our traditional customs become associated with the Church, or with some historical event, that their true origin and antiquity are often overlooked altogether.

Some of our existing customs, nevertheless, bear clear marks of their long pedigree. We owe to the Rev. W. H. Seddon, late Vicar of Painswick, some very interesting information about Painswick Feast, which now takes place on the Sunday nearest to September 19th. Here the old custom of "clipping the Church" is kept up. After a procession through the streets, the children join hands right round the church and advance and retreat three times, as in some country dances or in the children's game "Nuts and May."(2) On this day also most of the inhabitants of the village bake a "puppy-dog pie." This is traditionally supposed to have been a real pie made of cooked puppies at one time, but it is now a round cake with almond paste on top and a small china dog inside.

This simple and pleasant celebration has been carried on intermittently for centuries, and Mr. Seddon believes it to be a direct descendant of the ancient pagan Festival of the *Lupercalia*. Painswick was once a Roman settlement inhabited by the families of soldiers stationed in the adjacent camp, and the shopkeepers and others who served them. The Festival of the *Lupercalia* may well have been carried on there, since it was already ancient in the time of the Roman occupation of Britain, and was described by Cicero as "instituted before civilisation and laws existed." It was a festival of youth, the feast of Lycian Pan who protected the flocks from wolves. The rites included a sacred dance round the altar and the sacrifice of goats and young dogs. The *Luperci*, the youths who performed the sacrifice, dressed themselves in the skins of goats and afterwards rushed through the streets of the village, striking every woman they met with thongs of goat-skin.

Mr. Seddon considers that the church-clipping ceremony is a Christianised survival of the *Lupercalia*. He thinks that the actual clipping represents the dance round the altar and the once real puppy-dog pies the sacrifice of dogs. It used formerly to be the custom after the clipping was over for the children to rush down the road to the old Vicarage crying "Highgates! Highgates!" a word of which no one knew the meaning but which was traditional. This part of the ceremony is now obsolete, but Mr. Seddon believes that it sprang from a memory of the rush of the *Luperci* through the streets, and that the word itself is a corruption of the Greek *aig-aïtis*, from *aig*, a goat, and *aïtis*, an object of love.

If his theory is correct, we have here one of the oldest and most interesting rites in the country. It must have been handed down from generation to generation long after all understanding of its meaning had completely passed away, and have been incorporated at some early period with the Church Feast. When Mr. Seddon first went to Painswick he found the custom had lapsed for some years, but the older people remembered it clearly from their childhood days, and from their detailed accounts he was able to revive it in its present form.

It has been suggested by several writers that the Helston Furry is also Roman in origin, and is a survival of the *Floralia* once held in Rome in honour of the goddess Flora. It is pointed out that the Furry, like the *Floralia*, takes place in May, that the two rites are similar in some respects, and that the word "Furry," of which no one knows the precise meaning, may well be a corruption of "Flora." Against this theory it may be urged that the influence of the Roman conquerors was probably not very strong in the remote district we now call Cornwall, that "Furry" may come from the Celtic *feur*, a fair, as easily as from Flora, and that the present-day ceremonies show clearly marked traces of the ancient spring festivals once held all over Europe, in countries outside as well as within the Roman Empire. But Roman or native, the Helston Furry is undoubtedly pre-Christian, and its great interest for us to-day lies at once in the antiquity of the rites and the fresh gaiety and vigour with which they are carried out.

Local legend connects it with St. Michael, the patron saint of the parish, but the words of the Furry Song distinctly associate it with rejoicings at the return of summer. The chorus runs:

> And we were up as soon as any day O
> And for to fetch the summer home,
> The summer and the May O.
> For the summer is a come O
> And the winter is a go O.

"Fetching the summer home" in the form of green branches and flowers was once an important part of all May-day celebrations (4). In his *Anatomy of Abuses*, published in 1583, Stubbes tells us how

6

"Against Maie every parish, town and village assemble themselves together, bothe men, women and children, olde and young, even all indifferently: and either goyng all together or deuidying themselves into companies, they goe some to the woodes and groves, some to the hilles and mountaines, some to one place some to another; where they spende all the night in pastimes, and in the mornyng they returne, bringing with them birch bowes and braunches of trees to deck their assemblies withall."

This pleasant custom still prevails at Helston on May 8th, though the inhabitants do not spend all the night in the open as their ancestors did. The green branches are brought in early in the morning and every house is decorated with them. The day that follows is a general holiday and includes a fair as well as other delights, and usually ends with a ball. The most important event, of course, is the dancing through the streets which begins at seven o'clock with what used to be called the Maidservants' Dance. At half-past ten the children dance with willow-branches in their hands, and at noon the Invitation Dance begins. For this the men wear morning dress and buttonholes of flowers, and the women wear their prettiest summer frocks and bunches of lilies of the valley. Some years ago it was suggested that in these democratic days other forms of dress should be allowed, but the townspeople greatly resented the change, and the more formal clothes are once again necessary.

The dance itself is simple but it has one very interesting feature. As the couples swing through the streets, they pause to knock at every door; where a door stands open, they dance right through the house, into the garden or yard at the back, and then into the street again. The men bow and the women curtsey to anyone they meet in hall or corridor and, having thus brought the luck of the summer to the family by their presence, they dance away to the next house whose door stands open in invitation. The Helston Furry is not a church festivity, as so many of our old customs are, but a civic celebration in which the whole town takes part, from the town officials who usually lead the mid-day dance down to the youngest school-boy who shares in the children's dance and has a special holiday granted to him for this most important day in the town's year.

At Kingsteignton, in Devon, the decorated carcass of a lamb is carried in procession through the streets every Whit Tuesday, and is afterwards roasted in the open air. Sports and games are held while it is cooking. This is the remains of a very old custom which formerly took two days. A living ram-lamb used to be drawn about on Whit Monday in a cart covered with garlands of lilac and laburnum, and everyone who met it was asked to contribute something towards the cost of the ceremony. On the following day the animal was killed and roasted whole, and slices of the meat were sold cheaply to the poor of the parish. The origin of this custom is now forgotten by most of those who take part in it, but an old local tradition ascribes it to a pagan sacrifice in thanksgiving for the gift of water. At some remote period before Christianity was introduced into Devonshire, the village suffered from a lack of water. The people prayed to their gods for help, and at once a new spring rose in a meadow near the river. According to a writer in *Notes and Queries*, the spring was known as Fair Water and never ran dry, even in the hottest summer. A ram was offered in thanksgiving, and this sacrifice, annually repeated at Whitsuntide, is supposed to be the origin of the present custom.

Not far away, at Holne, another ram sacrifice used to be held on May-day morning. The young men met at dawn in the Ploy Field, in the centre of which stands a large granite menhir. From there they went to the moor and chose a ram-lamb which they ran down and brought back in triumph to the Ploy Field. It was fastened to the menhir, its throat cut so that its blood watered the stone and the ground beneath, and the carcass was then roasted whole, just as it was, in its wool and hide. At noon the young men scrambled for slices of the meat which were supposed to bring good luck, and the day ended with dancing, games and wrestling. It seems probable that this custom, which is now obsolete, was a more primitive form of the Kingsteignton ram-roasting, the sacrifice in this case being made to the menhir itself which, like many of these ancient standing-stones, was an object of worship for the local people.

The Horn Dance which takes place at Abbot's Bromley on the Monday after September 4th is another curious survival with a very long history. One explanation of this annual celebration is that it commemorates the restoration to the

5 The fool, with boggons carrying hoods, singing a toast

6 Smoking the fool outside the church

THE HAXEY HOOD GAME, LINCOLNSHIRE

7 Bringing the Yule Log, Penshurst Place, Kent

villagers of certain lost forest rights in the reign of Henry III, but the character of the dance itself points to its being very much older. Archbishop Theodore would certainly have disapproved of it, had he ever seen it, for here we have male dancers representing animals and carrying with them the skulls of reindeer whose branching antlers spring above the dancers' heads in a very realistic manner (3). That these skulls should be those of reindeer is exceedingly curious, for the dance itself appears to be a ritual reproduction of a hunt, and since the purpose of hunting dances was to bring success to the hunters by imitative magic, the quarry in such performances always represented an animal known to the people, and one which they might reasonably expect to capture in their own district. Reindeer have been extinct in England for so long that their very memory has died out, and unless through the agency of some Norse settler who knew reindeer in his original home, it is hard to see how these six skulls became the centre of a folk-custom on the edges of Needwood Forest. They were certainly in use in the seventeenth century, for Plot mentions them in his *Natural History of Staffordshire*, which was published about 1680. The same heads, now dark and polished with age and mounted on wooden handles, are kept during the year in the church tower and are brought out every September for the annual festivity.

The six principal dancers represent the deer, and carry their reindeer skulls pressed against their chests so that their heads and shoulders are surrounded and over-topped by the antlers (3). They line up opposite each other in the Market Place and dance to the music of an accordion and a triangle. With them are the two musicians, a man dressed as Robin Hood, another representing Maid Marion, a Fool in cap and bells, and a man with a crossbow and arrows. All are dressed in quaint flowered clothes of red and green, and Robin Hood is mounted on a hobby-horse whose jaws are snapped in time with the music. As soon as this first dance is over the deer-men run down the street, and the hunters run after them, led by the hobby-horse whose rider cracks his whip, while the bowman pretends to shoot his arrows at the escaping quarry. This is the beginning of a journey right round the scattered parish. Every farm and homestead within its boundaries is visited, and the dance is performed in road or garden before most of them. By the time the day is ended the dancers and their companions have walked, run and danced over some twenty miles of country which, considering the great weight of the horns and the cumbersome nature of such things as accordions and hobby-horses, is no mean achievement.

Men masquerading as animals are, or were until fairly recently, to be seen in several other districts. At Kingscote in Gloucestershire the Christmas Wassaillers used to be accompanied by a man wearing a sack and having his head thrust into the hollowed-out head of a bull. A writer in *Dorset Up Along and Down Along* describes how at Shillingstone

"The Bull, shaggy head with horns complete, shaggy coat, and eyes of glass, was wont to appear, uninvited, at any Christmas festivity. None knew when he might or might not appear. He was given the freedom of every house and allowed to penetrate into any room, escorted by his keeper. The whole company would flee before his formidable horns, the more so as towards the end of the evening, neither the Bull nor his keeper could be certified as strictly sober. The Christmas Bull is now obsolete, but up to forty years ago, he was a recognised custom."

The Hodening Horse did not invade the local houses in quite so free a manner, but he went round the village with a band of men and boys and leapt and pranced very spiritedly before the open doors. He wore a white sheet which covered most of his body, and a horse's head whose jaws opened and shut on hinges and could be made to snap in a very ferocious way. Hodening, which has not long died out, and which is still rememberd by many people not far beyond middle age, was a winter custom, taking place at Christmas in some districts, and on All Souls' Day or Eve in others. At Reculver only men who worked with horses during the year were allowed to take part; the strongest man of the party represented the horse and carried a wooden head, with large nails for teeth, on a pole. He was covered by a horse-cloth, wore reins and a bridle, and carried one of his companions on his back. The horse-man and his followers visited the farms in the neighbourhood and were given ale and other gifts. In the Welsh variant of this custom, known as Mari Lwyd, the skull of a horse was carried round to the houses, and largesse was demanded by its bearers at each one.

In Cheshire hodening took place on All Souls' Day and the hodening band went round with the Soulers. Here we have a clear example of a heathen custom grafted upon a later Christian one—the pagan horse, with its connection with ancient fertility rites and the horse-sacrifices of Romans and Norsemen which took place about this time, and the Christian Soulers commemorating the dead on All Souls' Day. In pre-Reformation times, men went through the streets on November 2nd, asking for prayers for the faithful departed and collecting money for Masses to be said for their intention. Souling was a relic of this pious custom. In Staffordshire, where it is no longer practised, the Soulers' song ran

> Soul-day, Soul-day,
> We've been praying for the soul departed;
> So pray good people, give us a cake,
> For we are all poor people, well known to you before;
> So give us a cake for charity's sake,
> And our blessing we'll leave at your door.

In Cheshire and parts of Shropshire the children still go from house to house on All Souls' Day, singing,

> Soul! Soul! for a soul-cake!
> I pray you, good missis, a soul-cake!
> An apple, a pear, a plum or a cherry,
> Or any good thing to make us all merry.
> One for Peter, two for Paul,
> Three for Them that made us all.

The cakes they ask for are no longer made, and they are rewarded with pennies or sweets instead. Both giver and receiver have forgotten that the gift was not originally intended for the singers, but for the souls in Purgatory who needed human help because they could no longer help themselves. It is only of recent years that souling has been left to the children; forty or fifty years ago, the Soulers were grown men, and every household baked a special batch of soul-cakes to give them on their rounds. That both they and the people they visited had long since lost sight of the Catholic origin of the custom did not prevent its being carried out with unabated vigour every year; and along with the Soulers went that representative of a much older and more completely forgotten faith, the Hodening Horse. He also appeared in the Soul-Caking Play which was acted in several Cheshire villages up to the outbreak of the Great War, and is still acted at Comberbach. This is the local version of the Mumming Play which is here given at Hallow-tide instead of at Christmas, as in most other counties. It is the only version of this ancient play which includes a horse; at Comberbach the character is called the Wild Horse and is described as a descendant of Marbury Dun, a famous racer who really lived, and is buried in the grounds of Marbury Hall.

The Haxey Hood Game (5, 6), which is played on January 6th, is an obviously ancient custom to which a more modern explanation has become attached in an attempt to explain the use of the word "hood." According to local tradition, a certain Lady Mowbray who lived in the thirteenth century was riding to church one Christmas Day, and lost her scarlet hood in a high gale. Twelve labourers rushed after it and rescued it for her, and as a reward for this ready courtesy she gave a piece of land to the village, the rent of which was to provide a hood to be contended for every Christmas Day by twelve men dressed in scarlet jerkins and velvet caps. A piece of land in the village is still known as the Hoodlands, and though the principal players do not now appear in thirteenth-century caps and jerkins, they do wear something scarlet on their shirts and in their flower-bedecked hats.

There are, however, certain details of the Hood Game which point to a far earlier origin than the thirteenth century. If Lady Mowbray did give the Hoodlands, she may have given it for a game with which she was already familiar and which was old in her time. The "hood" which is played for can never have resembled anything she ever wore, for it is not a hood at all, but twelve pieces of tightly rolled canvas, and a thirteenth roll of leather. It has been suggested that the word is derived from Old Danish *huid*, a head, and when the rest of the custom is examined, it seems quite possible that the contest is a relic of that scramble for the meat of a sacrificed animal which we have already seen at Holne, the leather roll representing the head which was always the most sacred part of the dedicated beast.

The players are known as boggons, and are led by the King Boggon who carries a bundle of thirteen willows bound by thirteen willow bands as a rod of office. With them goes a Fool with a blackened face who wears parti-coloured clothes and has strips of paper hanging down his back. Before the actual game begins the whole company, led by the King

8　A Christmas masque in the Banqueting Hall, Haddon Hall

From a lithograph by Joseph Nash

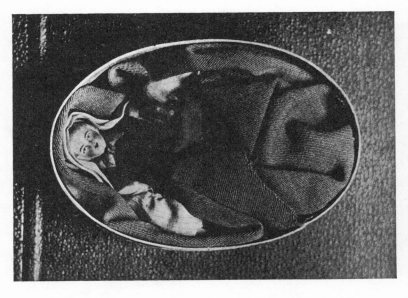

10 A wassail box, with effigies of Mary and the Christ Child,

9 Effigy of a boy bishop, Filey Church, Yorkshire

Boggon, march down to an old stone outside the church. On this the Fool stands and recites the story of Lady Mowbray's hood; while he is doing so, the paper strips on his back are set alight and a paper fire is lit at his feet (5). This custom of smoking the Fool was formerly found in several other places and is undoubtedly a relic of ancient sacrifice. At Haxey it was probably offered at the Winter Solstice and transferred in a modified form to the Christian festival of Christmas and, later, after the change in the calendar, to Old Christmas Day, January 6th.

When the smoking of the Fool is completed, the boggons march to a common on the hill and the contest begins. They stand at widely separated points in a large circle; the King and the villagers stand in the middle. The King throws one of the canvas hoods and the men in the centre rush after it. Whoever gets hold of it tries to get beyond the circle of waiting boggons; if he does so, that hood is dead and out of the game, but if he fails, it is returned to the King and thrown again. When all the canvas hoods are disposed of, the leather hood is thrown, the outer circle closes in, and the game spreads from the common right through the village. The three final goals are the three inns, each of which has a band of supporters who struggle to bring the hood to the chosen house. When at last it is safely inside the King's Arms, the Duke William or the Carpenters' Arms, the game is over, and nothing further remains but the celebration of victory.

Chapter II

THE CHRISTMAS SEASON

CHRISTMAS DAY is the greatest of all Christian festivals but it is not the oldest, and was not universally observed on December 25th until the fourth century. The Feast of the Epiphany was instituted much earlier, and until A.D. 325 the Nativity and the Adoration of the Magi were celebrated together in many places. But if its pagan ancestry be taken into account, the December festival is very old indeed. The Winter Solstice, so soon to be followed by lengthening days and the faint promise of spring, was a natural occasion for rejoicing, and from very early times it had been kept almost everywhere with ritual games and dancing, and sacrifices to the sun-god. In the North especially, where winter is hardest, it expressed all men's longing for light and warmth and the return of vegetation to the fields and woods. The Scandinavian Yule, from which so many of our older Christmas customs sprang, was a sun festival, when the Yule log was lit once more, and a boar's head was eaten in honour of the golden-bristled Sun-Boar. Mithras, whose cult resembled Christianity in so many ways, was supposed to have been born at the Winter Solstice and the birthday of Attis, the Phrygian sun-god, was kept on December 25th. The Roman *Saturnalia* began on December 17th and continued for about seven days. Saturn was originally a vegetation god, and his worshippers honoured him not only by a period of wild licence when master and slave changed places and ordinary laws were suspended, but also by a family celebration when each household sacrificed its sucking-pig, gifts were exchanged and laurels and evergreens hung on the walls. This great winter festival of fire and light, of new beginnings and lengthening days, was so deeply enshrined in the hearts of the people that they could never have been persuaded to give it up entirely. The Church therefore adopted and sanctified it by celebrating Our Lord's birth on December 25th, and thus swept away the old sun-worship and substituted that of the Holy Child.

In mediaeval times the holiday lasted for twelve days and

included our present New Year's Day and Twelfth Night. The Venerable Bede, in his chronological works, wrote of Christmas as the beginning of the year, and this manner of reckoning continued for some centuries, to the occasional confusion of those who study ancient documents and charters. The Roman year, governed by the Julian Calendar, began as our modern years do, in January, but the early English Church was unwilling to date the years of grace from a day so closely associated with heathen rites. The Calends of January, even though sanctified by the Feast of the Circumcision, had too pagan a flavour to be altogether acceptable to pious Christians, and the holy day of the Nativity seemed to them a much more appropriate beginning. Uniformity in dating did not come in until long afterwards; from the twelfth century to the eighteenth the English year began on Lady Day, and it was not until the adoption of the Gregorian Calendar in 1752 that England definitely returned to the ancient beginning on January 1st. Once it had been established, Christmas easily overshadowed the lesser dates near it, but the old New Year customs were still kept up, and the whole twelve days passed in a happy mixture of pagan survivals, religious ceremonies, and general rejoicings.

Almost all our existing Christmas customs have a long and interesting history. Houses were decorated with evergreens from the beginning, as they had been formerly for the northern Yule and the Roman *Saturnalia*. In his *Survey of London* Stow tells us that

". . . against the feast of Christmas every man's house, also their parish churches, were decked with holme, ivy, bayes and whatsoever the season afforded to be green. The conduits and standards in the streets were likewise garnished: among the which I read that in the year 1444, by tempest of thunder and lightning, towards the morning of Candlemas Day, at the Leadenhall, in Cornhill, a standard of tree, being set up in the midst of the pavement, fast in the ground, nailed full of holme and ivie for disport of Christmas to the people, was torne up and cast downe by the malignant spirit (as was thought), and the stones of the pavement all about were cast in the streets, and into divers houses, so that the people were sore aghast at the great tempests."

15

The "standard of tree" would, in any case, have been taken down a few hours later, for the ecclesiastical Christmas season ends at Candlemas, when all decorations must be removed from the churches. In houses also they were taken down, and it is still thought to be very unlucky in country districts to leave them hanging after that date.

Holly was always the favourite evergreen at this time, but ivy, yew, and rosemary were freely used, and occasionally cypress was included in spite of its mourning associations. Mistletoe was hung in houses but never in churches, where it was forbidden as a heathen plant. In *Popular Antiquities* Brand says an old sexton of Teddington told him it was once hung in the church there by mistake, and the clergyman ordered its instant removal as soon as he saw it. But in York at one time it received full honour. It was ceremonially carried to the Cathedral on Christmas Eve and laid upon the high altar, after which a universal pardon and liberty for all was proclaimed at the four gates of the city for as long as the branch lay upon the altar. To the Scandinavians mistletoe was sacred both as the instrument of Baldur's death and as the plant of peace under which enemies were reconciled, and the existence in this one district of so unusual a custom is probably due to the fact that York was for nearly a hundred years the capital of the Scandinavian Kingdom founded by Halfdan in 875.

Christmas trees were known in Northern Europe long before they were introduced into England in the middle of last century. Some German merchants living in Manchester are said to have set up the first tree in this country, and after Prince Albert started the custom at Windsor in 1841, it rapidly became popular wherever there were children to be delighted by the lovely sight of dark fir branches hung with bright coloured globes and blazing with candles and tinsel stars. In some country districts the older kissing-bough can still be seen hanging from the ceiling of cottage rooms at Christmas time. Iron hoops bent into the form of a crown are covered with greenery and decorated with apples and lighted candles. Usually a bunch of mistletoe is fixed to the underside, and in the North of England small presents are hung from it on long streamers of coloured ribbon.

Father Christmas, or Santa Claus, is really St. Nicholas who has inherited some of the attributes of Woden, particularly

11   The Eton Montem Ceremony, *ca.* 1820

From a contemporary coloured engraving

12 Midnight Service on February 14 at Norham-on-Tweed for the blessing of
the river-salmon net fishery

13 Bringing in the boar's head at The Queen's College, Oxford

those of riding or driving through the sky and of bringing gifts in darkness. Woden was thought to reward those who specially honoured him at Yule, and when it was no longer lawful to believe in him, the people transferred his legend to the generous and extremely popular St. Nicholas. He was Bishop of Myra in the fourth century and suffered imprisonment during Diocletion's persecution. After his death he became the patron saint of children, particularly scholars, and also of sailors, widows and virgins. Two of the best-known of his many legends specially marked him as the children's protector and the dispenser of gifts. He is said to have miraculously restored three schoolboys to life after they had been murdered by an innkeeper who hid their dismembered bodies in a pickling tub. On another occasion he heard that three young girls of his native town, Patara, were threatened with dishonour because of their father's extreme poverty. He saved them by going secretly to the house during the night and dropping three bars of gold through the window, thus providing them with dowries and enabling them to marry honourably. In Czechoslovakia he still appears as the Bishop he really was, but further north the old tradition was too strong. He became the ageless Father Christmas who rides, like Woden, through the clouds, and brings his gifts from the Far North in a sledge drawn by a team of reindeer.

On St. Nicholas' day, December 6th, the Boy Bishop was formerly elected in most cathedrals and in a number of parishes and grammar schools. The choristers or scholars chose one of their number to act as their Bishop from December 6th to Holy Innocents' Day, December 28th. During this period, he wore episcopal vestments and celebrated all but the most sacred services of the Church. If he died during his term of office, he was buried with full episcopal honours, and in Salisbury Cathedral there is a monument to one such child prelate which bears the effigy of a boy in bishop's vestments. The other children took the part of the lesser clergy; however strange the custom may now seem to us, there is no evidence of any irreverence in these ceremonies, either in intention or in fact, and the children carried out their duties in a seemly and efficient manner. In 1299 Edward I., then on his way to Scotland, heard a Boy Bishop sing vespers in his chapel at Heton and rewarded him and his followers with forty shillings, a considerable sum in those days. Processions through the streets were held during the child's season of office, and substantial presents were made to the little Bishop by householders and others. In some cases part of the money so collected was given to the church or cathedral funds, and in the records of Great Dunmow there are two entries in Tudor times of sums "recevyd of the bysshop at Seynt Nicolas tyme". On Holy Innocents' Day, the Boy Bishop was expected to preach a sermon, and in the Statutes of St. Paul's School, 1518, we read:

> "All these children shall every Childermas Daye, come to Pauli's Churche, and hear the Childe-bishop sermon: and after he be at hygh masse, and each of them offer a 1d to the Childe-bishop, and with them the maisters and surveyors of the scole."

This custom, which dates at least from the ninth century, was forbidden by Henry VIII in 1542, and after a temporary revival in Queen Mary's reign, was finally abolished in the time of Elisabeth. Traces of it lingered on for many years in the old Montem ceremony at Eton (11). This school, in common with many others, once had its Boy Bishop, and when that was forbidden, a Captain was elected instead, his followers being dressed as soldiers instead of priests. The Montem ceremony took place every two years at one time, and later was held triennially; before 1759 it took place on the first Tuesday in Hilary term, and was then changed to Whit Tuesday. The elected Captain and his supporters went in procession to Salt Hill, where a boy "chaplain" and a clerk read Latin prayers, after which the chaplain kicked the clerk down the hill. This part of the ceremony, which was undoubtedly a burlesque survival of the Boy Bishop rite, was given up after Queen Charlotte had objected to it as irreverent and unseemly. Before the procession started, the Saltbearers, two boys dressed in white or fancy dress, and their scouts, went through the town offering salt to all they met, and received money in return. The sums so collected went to the Captain and often amounted to a very considerable figure. *The Gentleman's Magazine* for June 1793 gives a long account of the Montem procession for that year, when George III, Queen Charlotte, and their children were present and "the collection for the benefit of the captain far exceeded all former ones; the sum spoken of amounts to near £1,000." Eton Montem was abolished in 1847, but not without a great deal of opposition from old Etonians and others interested in this time-honoured survival from the school's past.

In 1899 Boy Bishop ceremonies were inaugurated at Berden by the Rev. H. K. Hudson, and were held annually until 1937, when he left the parish. The present Vicar has not continued them, and it seems unlikely that this ancient custom will be revived now in any other district.

Another saint's day formerly associated with Christmas was St. Thomas' Day, December 21st. The saint had no association with the festival, but the day itself is the Winter Solstice, and a Staffordshire rhyme calls it

> St. Thomas Grey, St. Thomas Grey
> Longest night and shortest day.

Until quite recently women went "a-Thomassing" or "a-gooding," going from house to house to collect wheat with which to make a Christmas batch of cakes and bread. The usual contribution from each householder was a pint or a quart of wheat, which was taken to the miller to be ground into flour without charge. In return for these gifts the donor received a sprig of holly or mistletoe. In Staffordshire the clergyman also gave each woman a shilling, and in some parishes a collection called St. Thomas' Dole was made in church on the Sunday nearest December 21st. Thomassing or "curning", as it was called in Cheshire, was kept up until well within living memory.

Boar's head was often eaten at Christmas time and was always the principal dish wherever it was served. It was brought to table with great ceremony, usually on a gold or silver dish carried by the chief cook, and heralded by the sound of trumpets. This custom is undoubtedly a relic of paganism. The boar was sacred to Celt and Norseman alike; his flesh was the food of the heroes of Valhalla, and vows were sometimes taken on the boar's head at the Yuletide feast. At Hornchurch until quite recently a boar's head was provided every year by the lessee of the tithes. It was garlanded with bay-leaves and carried in procession on the afternoon of Christmas Day to a field near the church, where it was wrestled for by the people of the township.

The ceremony of the Boar's Head is observed every year at The Queen's College, Oxford, according to the custom of centuries (13). As soon as the Provost and Fellows have taken their seats at the high table and Grace has been said, the head is brought in on a silver basin given by Sir Joseph Williamson in 1668. It is decorated with sprigs of rosemary, bay and holly, and has an orange between the front teeth. Four servants carry the basin; before them goes the chief singer, and behind come the choir singing the refrain of the Boar's Head Carol. As the procession moves slowly up the hall, it halts three times to allow the chief singer to sing a verse of the carol; finally the head is placed on the table, and the Provost presents the chief singer with the orange from the boar's teeth, and the sprays of rosemary and bay are distributed amongst the guests.

This ceremony is known to have existed in the early sixteenth century and is probably very much older. The Carol was included in a collection printed by Wynkin de Worde in 1521. In the early days of the University, students only went home once a year, during the Long Vacation when they were wanted to help with the harvest. During the other vacations they remained in College, and Christmas festivities were provided for them there. Rice-Oxley suggests in *Oxford Renowned* that the Boar's Head ceremony continued at the Queen's College because its students were mainly north-countrymen whose homes were too far away for them to travel there in the short vacations, even when it became customary for the men of other colleges to do so. There is also a Boar's Head Dinner at Merton College. It is eaten on November 20th, but in this case the head is not a real one, but a confection of meats modelled in the form of a boar's head.

Christmas puddings as we know them were not eaten until about 1670, and first appeared as a stiffened form of the earlier plum porridge. This was a concoction of meat-broth, raisins, wine, fruit-juice and spices, the whole thickened with brown bread and served in a semi-liquid state at the beginning of the meal. Mince pies were well known by the end of the sixteenth century and contained mutton or neats' tongues, chicken and eggs, as well as the usual fruit and spice. Turkey appeared on Christmas tables about 1542 and gradually superseded the more magnificent dishes of our ancestors—swans, bustards, and peacocks dressed in their feathers and with gilded beaks. Hone in his *Table Book*, quoting from the *Newcastle Chronicle* for January 6th, 1770, describes a pie made for Sir Henry Grey by his housekeeper at Howick and sent to him in London. It

14 The waits in the snow, from a Victorian song-cover

15 Child carol-singers
By Phiz (Hablot K. Browne)

16 Carol-singers seen from inside
the house

17 The Marshfield Mummers, Gloucestershire: The Kill

18 The Pace-egging play, Midgley, Halifax. The doctor attends
the wounded warrior

contained four geese, two turkeys, four wild ducks, two rabbits, two curlews, seven blackbirds, six pigeons, four partridges, six snipe, two woodcock, and two neats' tongues. The pastry was made with two bushels of flour and twenty pounds of butter. In the same volume Hone gives the Christmas menu for 1800 at the Bush Inn in Bristol. It included no less than 150 items, amongst them sixteen sorts of fish, and thirty-nine different birds, but curiously enough, neither Christmas pudding nor plum porridge.

Carol-singing began very, early both in churches and outside (14 16), and the very word now suggests Christmas to us, though carols were also sung at other times. The children who come round to our houses usually content themselves with "Good King Wenceslaus," or "Noel! Noel!" somewhat indifferently rendered, but there are many others, some of them old and very lovely. The Coventry Carol "Lully, lulla, thou little tiny child," has been sung since the time of Henry VI: in 1940 the city's undaunted choir sang it as usual in the ruins of their ancient Cathedral, destroyed in an air raid only a short time before. At King's College, Cambridge, nine sets of carols are sung every year on Christmas Eve; the chapel is lighted only with candles on this occasion, and the choir carry candles in their hands as they enter by the West door. Some of the traditional carols are the happiest of songs, like "I saw three ships come sailing in," with its nursery-rhyme rhythm, and "The Holly and the Ivy"; others, like "The Five Joys of Mary," are gentle and tender and stress the babyhood of Jesus. Sometimes extra and more secular verses were added by those who went round singing; in Durham, after one or two verses of "God rest you, merry gentlemen," the children sang:

> We do not come to your house to beg for bread and cheese,
> But we do come to your house to give us what you please;
> The merry time of Christmas is drawing very near,
> And 'tis tidings of comfort and joy!

In Worcestershire every carol ended with the refrain:

> I wish you a happy Christmas and a happy New Year,
> A pocket full of money and a cellar full of beer,
> And a good fat pig to last you all the year.

Up to the end of last century, the singers in the northern counties carried little figures of Our Lady and the Holy Child (10), and Yorkshire children can still be seen occasionally with a "milly-box" lined with sugar and oranges and containing two small figures. The word "milly" is a corruption of "My Lady"; in Cleveland the same box is called a "bessel cup," and the children say they are going "a-wassailling." In Gloucestershire bands of young people used to take round a great bowl of spiced ale during the Christmas holidays, singing:

> Wassail! Wassail! all over the town,
> Our toast it is white, our ale it is brown,
> Our bowl it is made of the maplin tree,
> We be good fellows all; I drink to thee.

In Cumberland the wassailing song asked for the gifts "we were wont to have in old King Edward's time." The Wassail Bowl was an important part of the Christmas feast, and also appeared at New Year and Twelfth Night. It contained "Lamb's wool," a mixture of ale, roasted apples, sugar and spice; sometimes eggs and thick cream and sippets of French bread were added as well. At Jesus College, Oxford, there is a magnificent wassail bowl of silver gilt which holds ten gallons and has a ladle holding half a pint.

The mumming play was once very general at Christmas, when bands of mummers visited the various houses of the village and gave their traditional performance in kitchen or hall. In Cheshire, as we have seen, it was given on All Souls' Day and was known as the Soul-Caking Play; in Lancashire Easter was the time and it was there called the Pace-Egging Play. In most other counties, however, it was a Christmas festivity, and at one time nearly every village in England could produce its troupe of mummers. This interesting old play is obviously very ancient and bears marked traces of a ritual origin. Whatever the version given, the central theme is always that of death and resurrection. The characters vary a little from place to place but three are always included, the two men who fight and the doctor who raises the vanquished from the dead (18). The outline of the play never varies. First comes an introduction spoken by one of the characters, who frequently represents Father Christmas and acts as leader of the troupe. In the Cheshire version he is simply known as the Letter-in. Then comes the principal incident, the fight followed by the death of one of the warriors and his restoration to life by the doctor. St. George was the original hero, but he now usually appears as King George, a change which came

22

about naturally during the reigns of the four Georges. His opponent is sometimes a Turkish Knight, sometimes simply a Champion. Frequently he varied with the national enemy of the moment. At Islip formerly he was the Royal Duke of Northumberland and in one Berkshire version he was Beau Slasher, a French Officer. Whatever his name, he is always defeated and killed, and then the Doctor revives him with pills or a black draught, the administration of which often affords an opportunity for much rough comedy and horseplay.

A number of minor characters, such as Beelzebub, or Happy Jack, Molly or Little Devil Doubt, supply the comic relief and the local colour; in sword-dancing counties the village team accompanies the players. None of these have any real connection with the main theme of the play, which seems to be based upon some primitive vegetation rite. The slain man may represent the Corn Spirit who dies in the seed and rises again in the corn, or he may commemorate the sacrificial victim offered at seed-time and harvest. Such sacrifices were made not only to propitiate the spiritual powers, but also, by releasing life through death, to give stronger life to the crops. The Doctor is probably a survival of the priest or medicine man who conducted the ceremony, and whose power and ritual acts were necessary to make the corn grow. In its present form the Play was acted in England at least eight hundred years ago, and is interesting not only for its probably pagan origin but also because it is the only example of pre-Reformation folk drama still living in this country.

The words of the different versions have been handed down orally by generations of simple labourers and farm-hands, most of whom could neither read nor write. Corruptions have naturally crept in, and words not locally understood have been changed to something more familiar or corrupted into mere nonsense. In the Comberbach Soul-Caking Play Beelzebub entered, saying

> In comes B-I-Elzebub,
> Upon my shoulders I carry my clog

until Mr. A. W. Boyd pointed out that the real word was "club." A clog is a more familiar object to a Cheshire labourer than a club, and the thing itself more easily obtainable; this particular corruption does not occur in southern counties where clogs are not so generally worn.

Many of the village plays are no longer given and are now a mere memory. The words of some have been taken down from the lips of the actors, and others who knew them, by ardent collectors who thus saved them before they perished altogether. But in some places the old play is still acted with unabated vigour. It can be seen at Christmas at Alderley in Cheshire, the only place in the county where it is acted at that season, and at Comberbach on All Souls' Day. It has been acted recently at Chipping Campden and at Broadway, Eynsham and Sunningwell. At Comberbach the costumes are modern; King George wears khaki and the Black Prince, his opponent, wears a spiked helmet and a bandsman's coat, and has his face blackened. At Longparish the mummers have strips of coloured material sewn all over their clothes with the ends hanging loose so that they flutter with every movement. An immensely tall headdress is surmounted by a large wreath from which streamers of paper hang down before and behind, completely covering the wearer's face (20, 21). The Overton mummers' dress is rather similar, but with longer streamers on the clothes, and towering mitre-like headdresses (19). Their faces are also covered by paper streamers, and their general appearance, like that of the Longparish troupe, is very striking and strongly reminiscent of primitive medicine men. Both these bands perform regularly at Christmas time; during·the day they go round to the principal houses, often acting on the lawns or by the roadside, and at night they visit the various inns of the district.

St. Stephen's Day, December 26th, was formerly the traditional day for blooding horses. It is better known to us now as Boxing Day, a name supposed to be taken from the earthen boxes in which the apprentices collected money from their masters' customers. Servants, also, journeymen and others received gifts at this time, as postmen and dustmen do to-day. According to *John Bull*, January 1st, 1837, the Foreign Office made a determined effort to stop the custom that year by sending round a circular to all the Embassies forbidding "the customary Christmas boxes to the messengers of the Foreign Department, domestic servants of Viscount Palmerston, foreign postmen, etc., much to the chagrin of the latter," but probably this, like other similar attempts, had very little effect. Innkeepers used to remit the charge for part of every meal, at this time, a pleasant habit now unfortunately quite obsolete.

19 The Overton Mummers in the snow, Hampshire

20 Little Johnny Jack, with dolls

21 King George

COSTUME OF LONGPARISH MUMMERS, HAMPSHIRE

22. The Bursar conducting the New Year needle and thread ceremony at The Queen's College, Oxford

At Drayton Beauchamp the villagers used to go to the Rectory on Boxing Day to receive as much bread, cheese and ale as they could consume from the Rector. This custom was known as Stephening; the gift was looked on as a right and, according to local tradition, when one clergyman refused to admit them, the people broke a hole through the roof and completely cleared both larder and cellar. In 1808 the Rev. Basil Wood was appointed to the living, and managed to persuade the villagers to accept an annual distribution of money instead of the traditional food and drink. When the Charity Commissioners were inquiring into various charities in 1834, many Drayton inhabitants gave evidence as to the antiquity of the custom and the Rector's clear duty in the matter, but they were unable to prove any legal right, and the practice lapsed for good and all. At Cumnor the tithepayers expected to receive bread and cheese and ale at the Vicarage on Christmas Day after evening service. The Vicar had to provide four bushels of malt for ale and small beer, half a hundredweight of cheese, and two bushels of wheat in the form of bread. Whatever was left over when the tithepayers had eaten their fill was given to the poor after the service next morning. Ecclesiastical feasts really begin after sunset on the previous day, so, although the meal was taken on December 25th, it seems evident that this also was a form of Stephening, and really belonged to St. Stephen's Day.

Chapter III

THE BEGINNING OF THE YEAR

As long as we continue to divide our lives into set periods of twelve months, giving each a number and reckoning the length of our lives by them, so long will New Year's Day be an important date for all of us, a sort of fresh start and an unofficial feast of beginning. Because of its pagan associations the early Christians observed the Calends of January as a strict fast, and January 1st was specially left out of the Christmas feast by the Second Council of Tours in 567. But such a beginning for the year could not long be kept up even by the most devout. A superstition deeply-rooted in the human mind everywhere demands that the start of anything shall be happy if the end of it is to be so, and a good year could not always be begun in sorrow and abstinence. In the eighth century the day was established as the Feast of the Circumcision, and religious sanction was thus given to the rejoicings which had never been stamped out amongst the generality of people. In Scotland and France New Year's Day now ranks even before Christmas in importance, and if it has not quite the same place in English affections, it is nevertheless marked by a number of customs, religious and otherwise, that are proper to it.

In nearly all churches a Watch Night Service is held on New Year's Eve, and the bells are pealed immediately after midnight. At Basingstoke a hymn is sung on the church tower as soon as the service is ended. Ships in port and at sea sound their sirens at twelve o'clock, and wherever people are gathered together toasts are drunk and good wishes exchanged. In the North of England the custom of first-footing is still kept up. A dark-haired man must be the first person to cross the threshold after midnight, and he should bring gifts with him, usually bread, coal and money, if the family is to be lucky during the year. Under no circumstances should a fair-haired man or a woman be the first to enter the house. Whether the underlying superstition is believed or not, the custom is firmly rooted in towns as well as villages, and careful arrangements are made beforehand to secure the services of a dark friend, who often makes the round of a number of houses before the night is over.

In Manchester and the surrounding district January 1st is observed as a general holiday, when all the shops are closed and no one works if he can possibly avoid it. Up to the beginning of this century, servants in Cheshire were given a holiday in Christmas week and were not expected to come back to work until January 2nd. Farmhands would never go to a fresh place on New Year's Day, as it was considered very unlucky to do so. This custom is now obsolete, but the New Year festival is still sufficiently observed to make it unusual for newly-engaged servants to arrive before the second day of the month.

At the Queen's College, Oxford, the Bursar gives every Fellow a needle threaded with coloured silk on January 1st, saying, "Take this and be thrifty" (22). This curious little ceremony is a French pun—*aiguille et fil*—on the name of Robert de Eglesfield, who founded the College in 1341. He was chaplain to Queen Philippa who became the first patron of the College, as the Queens Consort of England have been ever since. He provided for a Provost and twelve Fellows in honour of Our Lord and the Twelve Apostles, and ordered that they should wear crimson mantles, for Our Lord's Blood, and should sit at meals on one side only of the High Table, with the Provost in the middle, after the manner of traditional pictures of the Last Supper. The scholars were to wear tabards, and for this reason the eight senior students of the College are known to-day as Tabardars.

A very strange custom called Hunting the Mallard is kept up at All Souls College on January 14th at intervals of a hundred years. The explanatory legend says that when the foundations of the College were being laid in 1438 the workmen disturbed a mallard which rose suddenly from a drain and flew away. It is this bird which is hunted by the Fellows under the leadership of an elected Lord Mallard and six officers appointed by him. All are armed with staves and lanterns; the officers wear medals specially struck for the occasion showing the Lord Mallard and his assistants on one side and the bird on a long pole on the other. The whole company search throughout the College and over the leads, singing a ballad, the chorus of which runs

> O by the blood of King Edward,
> O by the blood of King Edward,
> It was a swapping, swapping Mallard.

No one knows which King Edward is meant, or what he has to do with it; perhaps he is the same king about whom the Cumberland wassaillers sang when they went on their rounds. The song itself seems to have been written at some time in the sixteenth century and may have replaced an earlier one.

In a letter dated January 15th, 1801, Bishop Heber[1] describes the hunt as he saw it in the small hours of that morning. He says:

"I write under the bondage of a very severe cold which I caught by getting out of bed at four in the morning to see the celebrations of the famous All Souls mallard feast. All Souls is on the opposite side of Radcliffe Square to Brazen Nose so that their battlements are in some degree commanded by my garret. I had thus a full view of the Lord Mallard and about forty Fellows in a kind of procession on the library roof with immense lighted torches, which had a singular effect. I know not if their orgies were overlooked by any uninitiated eyes exept my own: but I am sure that all who had the gift of hearing within half a mile must have been awakened by the manner in which they thundered their chorus, 'O, by the blood of King Edward.' "

It is not known why January 14th should be the chosen date nor why the hunt should take place only once a century. Its origin is very obscure; it has been suggested that the whole custom sprang from the finding of a seal marked with a griffin and the name of William Mallard, clerk, near the Warden's Lodgings in the seventeenth century. It is not clear who William Mallard was; judging from the age of his seal, he must have lived in the thirteenth century, before All Souls was built. It does not seem very likely that this chance find should have resulted in so curious a practice, and we know that the custom existed at least as early as 1632, for in that year Archbishop Abbot censured the College for a riot "in pretence of a foolish Mallard." The Mallard was last hunted in 1901 and the ceremony therefore does not fall due again for another sixty years. It was proposed to hold it during the Quincentenary celebrations in 1938, but for some reason the idea was abandoned.

At St. Ives in Cornwall the guise-dancers still perform in

[1] *Life of Heber*, by his Widow.

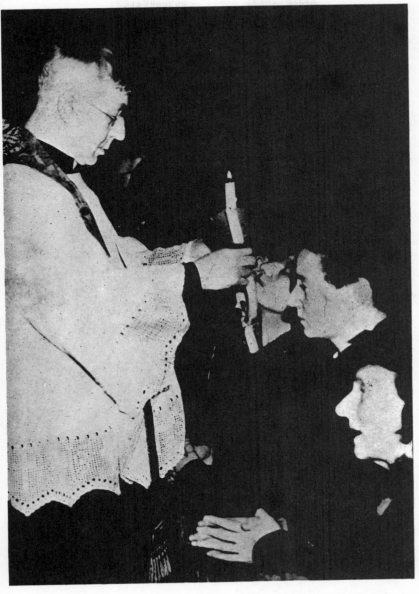

23 The ceremony of Blessing the Throat, at St. Etheldreda's Church,
Ely Place, London

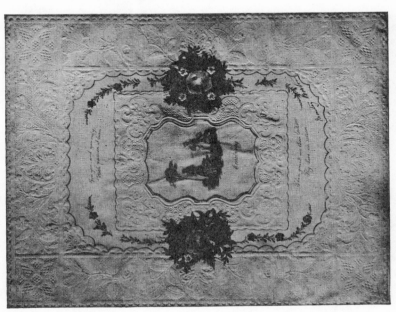

24, 25 Old lace Valentines of about a century ago

the streets during the first fortnight in January. This ancient New Year celebration, which dates from pre-Christian times, was once held almost everywhere; now it is rapidly dying out and even in St. Ives it is little more than a rather noisy jollification, the original meaning of which has been forgotten. The dance is a Processional and is given in the open streets by men whose faces are blackened, or who are otherwise disguised. In some places a man dressed as an animal used to accompany the performers. At Wainfleet in Lincolnshire as late as 1892 one man was dressed in skins and had a wisp of straw cut to resemble a pig's bristles in his mouth. In the Land's End district a man with a bullock's head over his own pranced and capered along with the regular dancers. Until quite recently in St. Ives the guisers entered the houses and performed all sorts of ridiculous antics in them. The householders took it all in good part, for these visits, like those of the Furry dancers, were thought to bring good luck. At Skipsea forty years ago troupes of young men with blackened faces ran through the village as soon as midnight had struck on New Year's Eve and chalked the date of the year on doors and gates and on the farm waggons. This also was supposed to be fortunate, and only those to whom the young men were hostile were left without a lucky chalk mark somewhere on their property.

The name "guisers" comes from the universal custom of disguising the performers in some way or other, either by blackening their faces or dressing them in some unusual manner. This desire for secrecy is found not only in the New Year processional dance, but also in nearly all the ancient ritual dances. Most Morris teams are accompanied by a black-faced Fool or "Dirty Bet," and all wear a special traditional dress. At Bidford the Morris captain wears a foxskin on his head with the tail hanging down behind, and this headdress used to be worn by one of the dancers in the old Plough Monday processions in Lincolnshire. In some villages formerly the names of the Sword- or Morris-dancers were never mentioned, though everyone knew who the men were. Mummers also blacked their faces, or covered them with strips of paper, as the Longparish and Overton men still do. The disguise was in fact an integral part of the performance and arose from the ritual nature of the dance or play, the men being for the time something quite other than their ordinary selves and performing

4*   29

magical acts, like the beheading in the Sword-dance or the seed-sowing in "Bean-setting," which have nothing to do with their everyday lives. It is interesting to note in this connection that in Northamptonshire the guisers used to be called "the witch-men."

On January 6th, the Feast of the Epiphany, a special service is held in the Chapel Royal, St. James's, in memory of the gifts of the Three Kings. The Lord Chamberlain in his robes, attended by the Yeoman of the Guard, comes to represent the King, and presents three purses in his name while the offertory is being read. Up to the time when George III's madness kept him from this and every other royal duty, the King himself came in state to the service and offered gold, frankincense and myrrh with his own hand. During the Regency the presentation was made by proxy and this has been done ever since, the traditional gifts being now changed to three purses containing money for the poor of the parish.

Twelfth Night falls on January 6th and marks the end of the Twelve Days of Christmas. In most houses Christmas decorations are taken down then or on the morning after. It is also Old Christmas Day, when the Holy Thorn of Glastonbury, faithful to the old Calendar, is said to blossom exactly at midnight. Little attention is now paid to Twelfth Night, but formerly it was a festival of great importance. In Gloucestershire, thirteen fires were lighted in the fields in honour of Our Lord and his Twelve Apostles. The fire named for Judas was stamped out immediately, and the others were allowed to burn out. The farmhands were given plum- or seed-cake, and cider. In Herefordshire the wassail-bowl was taken to the cow-byre and the cattle were toasted. Sometimes a cake with a hole in the middle was hung on the horns of an ox; if he tossed it behind him, the mistress of the house had it, if in front, it went to the bailiff or headman of the farm. A large plum-cake was often made with a bean in it, and whoever got the slice containing the bean was King for the day. Sometimes a pea was included also, and the finder was hailed as the Queen.

These cheerful customs are now quite obsolete, but the apple trees are still "wassailled" in Somerset and Devonshire. Bands of men go out to the orchards at night and fire their guns through the branches; cider is poured round the roots of the trees, and cake or toast soaked in cider is set in the fork.

The object of this ceremony is to urge the apple-trees to greater efforts in the coming year, and they are addressed as living beings in the traditional song which is sung during the proceedings. There are several versions of this song; the following is perhaps the oldest:

> Here's to thee, old apple-tree,
> Whence thou mayst bud, and whence thou mayst blow,
> Whence thou mayst bear apples enow!
> Hats full! Caps full!
> Three score bushels full!
> And my pockets full, too!
> Huzza! Huzza! Huzza!

At Carhampton and Roadwater the trees are wassailled on Old Twelfth Night, January 17th.

The Monday following January 6th is Plough Monday, a day on which ploughing matches are often held now. In Cambridgeshire and North Lincolnshire boys with blackened faces drag an old plough through the streets and demand money from the passers-by. As so often happens, the children here are the last guardians of a custom which once marked the beginning of the ploughing season. A decorated plough was dragged from house to house by the ploughmen who asked for money or other gifts. If they did not receive them, they ploughed up the lawn or the ground in front of the house. In Yorkshire the Sword-dancers went with them, and at Goathland the members of the sword-dancing team are still known as Plough Stots, the old local name for those who took the place of the oxen on this day. In Leicestershire the Morris dancers accompanied the ploughmen, and in many parts of the country a Mumming Play was given at this time. It differed from other Mumming Plays inasmuch as the victim was not St. George or a king but an old woman; it may possibly be the oldest version, since the Corn Spirit was generally thought to be feminine. Another character was Hopper Joe, who carried a basket and went through the motions of sowing seed.

The plough itself was called the Fool Plough, or in some cases the White Plough. The men who drew it were variously known as Plough Stots, Bullocks or Jacks. In Nottinghamshire they wore horse-brasses on their clothes, and coloured rosettes or streamers of ribbon were general. In *The Gentleman's Magazine* for December 1672 Dr. Pegge describes how

"On this day the young men yoke themselves and draw a plough about with musick, and one or two persons in antic dresses, like jack-puddings, go from house to house, to gather money to drink. If you refuse them, they plough up your dunghill."

Hutchinson, in his *History of Northumberland*, says "I have seen as many as twenty men in the yoke of one plough." The money collected was spent on drinking and feasting, but in pre-Reformation times a part of it went to pay for the Plough Light, a lamp kept burning in many churches through the year, and maintained by all the husbandmen of the parish.

The Feast of the Purification on February 2nd, usually known as Candlemas Day, was established in the fifth century and took the place of a Roman festival in honour of Februa, when torches and candles were carried about. It celebrates the Purification of Our Lady and the Presentation of Jesus at the Temple, and gains its second name from the old custom of carrying lighted candles in the churches during the service. In a Proclamation of Henry VIII's reign, dealing with the rites of the English Church, it is stated: "On Candelmas Daye, it shall be declared that the bearynge of candels is done in the memorie of Christe, the spirituall lyghte, when Simeon dyd prophecye, as it is redde in the churche that daye." Formerly every church distributed its blessed candles on February 2nd, and women who came to be churched at any time during the year carried lighted candles in their hands. These usages are no longer general, but in all Roman Catholic churches on this day candles are blessed and given to the congregation, so that during Mass the lights on the altar are reflected all down the aisles in the myriad flames of burning candles held by the worshippers. At Blidworth in Nottinghamshire a charming custom commemorates the Presentation at the Temple. A decorated cradle on rockers is placed near the altar, and the baby last baptised in the parish is laid in it and gently rocked for a few moments by the priest.

The following day, February 3rd, is the Feast of St. Blaise, patron saint of woolcombers. He was a Bishop of Dalmatia who suffered martyrdom in A.D. 316, his flesh being torn to pieces by sharp iron combs. Hence his connection with the woolcombers. His day was formerly a holiday for women, who dared not spin for fear of having their distaffs torn from them

26 Football in the streets of Barnet, *ca.* 1760
From a contemporary engraving

27 The Bells of St. Clement Danes, hung with oranges and lemons
Dedicated 1919. Destroyed by enemy action 1941

28 Yeomen of the Guard bearing the purses

29 Some of the recipients

THE KING'S MAUNDY MONEY AT WESTMINSTER ABBEY

by their neighbours and burnt. It was also a great feast in towns connected with the wool trade. A contributor to *County Folklore* (*Suffolk*) writes that up to the beginning of the nineteenth century, the woolworkers of Hadleigh had a procession in which a woman dressed as a shepherdess rode in a postchaise with a lamb in her lap. In the same volume an account dated February 3rd, 1777, tells how in Bury St. Edmunds

"This day, Munday, being the anniversary of Bishop Blaize, the same was observed in this town in a manner far surpassing anything of the kind ever seen. The Cavalcade consisting of between two or three hundred Woolcombers, upon Horses in uniforms, properly decorated. Bishop Blaze, Jason, Castor and Pollux, a band of musick, drums, colours, and everything necessary to render the procession suitable to the greatness of the Woollen Manufactory."

St. Blaise is chiefly remembered now as the patron saint of those who suffer from diseases of the throat. It is traditionally said that, while he was actually going to his death, he saved the life of a boy who was being choked by a fish-bone. He touched the lad's throat with his finger and the bone was at once dislodged. An old charm for removing obstructions of this kind, still found in country districts, is to hold the sufferer's neck and command whatever is causing the trouble to "move up and down" in the name of the martyred Bishop. Water which had been touched by some relic of the saint and blessed in his name was once widely used as a cure for throat troubles, and at St. Mary's Abbey, East Bergholt, St. Blaise's Water is still so blessed on his feast-day and sent to patients all over the world. At St. Etheldreda's Church in Ely Place the Benediction of the Throat is given at three services on February 3rd. Two long candles are blessed and dedicated to St. Blaise and joined together with ribbons in the form of St. Andrew's Cross. Those who suffer from throat troubles kneel while the ribbon cross is laid under their chins, and the afflicted part is gently touched with the end of the lighted candles (23). The priest says to each patient "May the Lord deliver you from the evil of the throat, and from every other evil," and then passes on to repeat the ceremony of healing with the next person.

In the last two or three years, Valentines, once so popular in this country, have appeared again in the shops a little before

February 14th. These little lace-edged cards, adorned with hearts and roses and richly sentimental verses (24, 25), were so general in Victorian times as to make almost as great an increase in the delivery of letters as Christmas cards do now. They were then, as now, a means of expressing preference, and were despatched by the sender to the person of his or her choice. Originally, however, it was much more a matter of luck. The young people met to draw lots for their sweethearts by means of billets on which were written the names of the girls and boys present. The chosen girl received gifts from her Valentine and wore the billet in her dress for some days afterwards. St. Valentine, priest and martyr, who died for his faith in A.D. 269 and was renowned for his chastity, would seem to have little connection with this custom, except that he was beheaded on February 14th, the eve of the festival of the *Lupercalia*. This, as we have already seen, was a feast of youth, which included the drawing of women's names from a box, and the striking of women with goat-thongs to make them fruitful. St. Francis de Sales and other holy men tried to abolish the choice of sweethearts by lot, and substituted billets bearing the names of saints whom the receivers were invited to imitate and honour in special ways. It is hardly necessary to say that this pious reform made very little difference to the general custom.

The gifts connected with Valentines made this saint's day very popular with children. In Pepys' *Diary* we read: "I find that Mrs. Pierce's little girl is my Valentine, she having drawn me; which I was not sorry for, it easing me of something more than I must have given to others." In Herefordshire the children used to go round the village in wreaths and ribbons singing,

> Good morrow, Valentine.
> Please to give me a Valentine.
> I'll be yours if you'll be mine.
> Good morrow, Valentine.

The Berkshire boys' rhyme in the nineteenth century was not perhaps so romantic, but showed a clearer understanding of the average adult's love of peace. It ran:

> Knock the kettle against the pan,
> Give us a penny if you can;

34

We be ragged and you be fine,
Please to give us a Valentine.
Up with the kettle and down with the spout.
Give us a penny and we'll get out.

In Norfolk the children rose very early and tried to catch some kindhearted person before sunrise. If any child could say "Good-morrow, Valentine," twice before he (or she) was spoken to, he was given a present, provided the sun had not yet risen; if it had, he could be refused on the ground that he was "sunburnt." Probably this time-limit was never very strictly observed, at all events by people who loved children.

On this day when, according to country lore, the wild birds choose their mates, marriage divination was often practised. A girl would pin bay leaves to the corners and centre of her pillow, and would then expect to dream of her future husband. Young people of both sexes wrote names on slips of paper which they rolled into clay and dropped the balls so made into bowls of water to see which name would rise first to the surface. The first person of opposite sex met in the morning was the Valentine in some districts; in others it was said that if a single girl met a man when she first went out, she would be married in three months, but if the first encounter was with another woman, she would not marry at all that year. In north-west Derbyshire only a few years ago, a girl who was not kissed or visited by her sweetheart was said to be dusty and was swept down with a broom or a wisp of straw, after which she had to cast lots with the other girls and draw the name of her future husband from among a number of names shaken up in an old hat.

At Norham-on-Tweed the river, the boats, the fishermen and the nets are solemnly blessed at about 11.45 p.m. on February 14th, a custom which has nothing to do with the usual celebrations of St. Valentine's Day. It is the opening ceremony of the Salmon Net Fishing season, and the benediction is given not for Norham only, but for the whole river and its net fisheries, of which there are thirty-eight. In the darkness of the February night, often in wild or snowy weather, the fishermen and people from both sides of the Border assemble at the ancient fishery of Pedwell for the service conducted by the Vicar of Norham (12). It is held just before midnight so as to allow the first boat of the season to be launched on the stroke of twelve o'clock. Some sort of service at the beginning of the fishing season was formerly usual wherever there were fishermen, and although the present custom at Norham is only about fifty years old, it probably replaces an older benediction which had been allowed to lapse.

Chapter IV

LENTEN CUSTOMS

THE decline in severity of the Lenten fast has caused a corresponding decline in the festival importance of Shrove Tuesday. It is now principally observed as the day on which we are accustomed to eat pancakes, though there is no longer any practical reason for doing so. In pre-Reformation times, however, all the eggs and butter left in the house had to be cleared up before Ash Wednesday, as they could not be eaten during Lent, and most of the remaining material went into the pancakes. In country districts the previous day is still sometimes called Collop Monday from the similar necessity of finishing up the stock of meat. Shrove Tuesday was the day on which the faithful went to confession before the holy season and were shriven; it was also the last opportunity for merry-making before Lent began, and was kept as a general holiday. Games and sports of every kind, cock-fighting and wrestling and the less reputable pastime of "thrashing the hen" were the order of the day; the schoolmaster received his "cockpenny" from the children, and was sometimes barred out of his own school by them. Street football was, and still is, played in a number of places. In Cornwall "Nickanan Night" was celebrated by all sorts of wild antics more or less tolerated by the quieter people as being of ancient custom. Women rubbed sooty hands on the faces of all they met; boys beat on the house-doors with clubs, carried away gates and knockers and threw water over everyone. The day's revelry everywhere was started by a morning bell and ended by another in the evening, after which Lent was considered to have begun in earnest.

The first bell is generally called the Pancake Bell and is still rung in many churches. In Cheshire it used to be called the Guttit Bell, in reference, perhaps, to the pancake-eating contests which followed. In York at one time the apprentices and journeymen had the right to enter the Minster and ring the bell, the cathedral being specially left open for them. So greatly was this privilege esteemed that when, in the seventeenth

century, Bishop Lake tried to put a stop to it, a serious riot
ensued and the Bishop himself was threatened with physical
violence. There can be little doubt that the bell was really
intended in the beginning to call the people to confession, but
for generations it has been regarded as the official opening of
the holiday and a signal to start making pancakes. At Olney
in Buckinghamshire, the housewives, as soon as they hear it,
race to the church with their frying-pans, tossing their pancakes as they run. Such pancakes as survive this perilous
journey are given to the bell-ringer. At Westminster School
the cook, preceded by a verger carrying the silver-topped mace,
takes his frying-pan at eleven o'clock to the Lower School and
tosses a pancake over the high iron bar which separates it from
the Upper School. The boys then scramble for it, and he who
secures it, or the largest part of it, is given a guinea. The
cook receives 10s. for his part in the affair. At one time all
the boys in the school took part in the scramble, but now
each form chooses a delegate to represent it.

Children still go a-shroving in many parts of the country,
and are usually given cakes, sweets or money instead of the
"piece of pancake, or a bit of bacon, or a little truckle cheese
of your own making" for which the old song asks. In 1925
Mr. Valentine Rickman of Durweston, Dorset, left £50 to
preserve this ancient custom in the village, the money being
held in trust by the Rector and Churchwardens and the
interest divided between the schoolchildren who go shroving
to at least three houses. Shrove Tuesday was sometimes called
Lin-Crock Day because the children brought broken crockery
with them and smashed it before the houses, after which the
householder came out and tossed a pancake for them. If they
were not given the desired gifts, they would throw these shards,
or possibly stones, against the door. Up to the end of last
century egg-shackling competitions were held in Cornwall and
Dorset. At St. Columb the eggs were hit against each other,
end on, until only the victor's egg remained unbroken. At
Powerscourt the same idea was carried out in a more polite
manner. The schoolchildren elected a committee and a judge,
and various prizes were given for the largest and smallest and
the brownest eggs. Then all were placed in a sieve and shaken
until they were cracked, and the owner of the last whole egg
received a prize. Here undoubtedly the schoolmaster's influence can be seen in this taming of a gloriously messy custom

30　The King's Maundy Money at the Banqueting Hall, Whitehall, 1777: the distribution at the tables

From a water-colour by S. H. Grimm

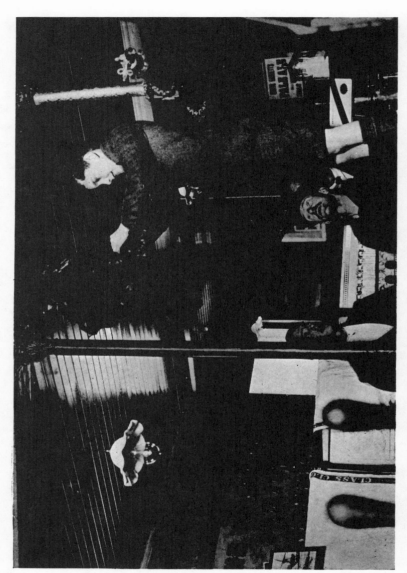

31 The Widow's Son Inn, Bromley. The memorial buns

which continued in its original form at St. Columb until it died out altogether.

Tideswell in Derbyshire is one of the few places where the old custom of barring out the schoolmaster is still kept up. Here the children ride round the village on long poles, taking it in turn to carry each other. Arrived at the school, they lock the door against the schoolmaster and refuse him entry. In this district the day is kept as a school holiday, so the point of the barring-out is now lost. Formerly, however, it was a serious matter, and the children would not give way until they had been promised at least a half-holiday. The boys of Bromfield School in Cumberland used to barricade the doors and defend them against the master with pop-guns and any other weapons they could find. If, in spite of this, he managed to get in, school went on as usual and specially heavy tasks were imposed on the defeated scholars but if, as frequently happened, he was unable to do so, the boys remained in charge for three days and only capitulated on agreed terms, which usually included the immediate holding of a football match and a cock-fight. This custom was almost universal in country districts and was no doubt taken in good part by the masters, who were thus left free to enjoy a compulsory holiday themselves. In Cheshire barring-out took place later in the year, either just before Easter or nine days before Christmas.

Street football (26) is played in a number of towns on Shrove Tuesday. It is a game which professional footballers would not easily recognise, for it has no rules and in some cases no definite goals. At Chester-le-Street it is played between the "up-streeters" and the "down-streeters," and most shops and houses take the precaution of barricading their windows while it is going on. At Ashbourne it begins on the Belper side of the town, and the Henmore brook and several lesser streams have to be crossed during the course of it. The goals are about three miles apart; long before the end of the game the players are plastered with mud from head to foot and dripping wet, but nobody minds, and the contest goes on more or less indefinitely until darkness falls.

At Atherstone the village street forms part of the main London-Holyhead road, and all traffic has to be diverted for the occasion. The ball is thrown from an inn window at three o'clock and the game rages up and down the street until time is called at five. One of the players then tries to hide the ball up his jersey and run away with it, hotly pursued by the others. If he succeeds, he has won the game, but if someone takes it from him, the proceeding is repeated until some stronger and faster runner manages finally to escape with it. At Sedgefield the church clerk and the sexton provide the ball, and the game is played between widely separated goals at the northern and southern ends of the village.

Football was formerly played in the street at Alnwick also, but so much damage was done that the game was transferred to a field known as The Pasture. Here some attempt is made to keep rules, though there are no set teams, the contest being between the men of St. Michael's and St. Peter's parishes. A committee receives the ball from the Castle porter and carries it to the field, preceded by the Duke of Northumberland's piper. The goals in this case are only about a quarter of a mile apart and are decorated with evergreens. As soon as the real game is over, the tenants compete for a money prize offered every year by the Duke to the first man who carries the ball across his boundaries, one of which is that not inconsiderable obstacle to progress, the River Aln. Here again, as at Ashbourne, much cheerful scrambling in mud and water takes place before the winner can deposit the ball on the right side of the boundary and claim his prize.

The Corfe Castle Shrove-tide football is particularly interesting because it maintains an old right of way. The famous Purbeck stone is quarried in this district, and on Shrove Tuesday the Ancient Company of Marblers holds its court at Corfe Castle. Apprentices are then admitted to the Company and pay the Wardens 6s. 8d. in money, a loaf, and two pots of beer as admission fee. No man can be admitted before he is twenty-one; according to the original articles of the Company only quarrymen's sons could become quarrymen, and this rule was strictly kept for several centuries. After the court meeting is over, a football is kicked along the old road towards Poole in order to keep open the way to the nearest large harbour from which the stone used to be shipped.

Hurling matches are played at St. Columb Major on Shrove Tuesday and on the preceding day, Quinquagesima Monday, at St. Ives. At St. Columb Major the game is played in the traditional way right through the town. This was formerly the case at St. Ives also, where it formed part of the celebrations of Feasten Monday, the patronal festival of the parish church falling on Quinquagesima Sunday. This is traditionally said to be the date on which St. Ia landed in Cornwall after she had fled from her Irish persecutors and crossed the sea on a leaf. Later, the match was held on the beach, the Mayor throwing the silver-coated ball always used here from the West Pier to the waiting crowds below. In 1939 it was unfortunately transferred to a public park and thus robbed of much of its old interest, though it is still as vigorous and devoid of obvious rules as ever.

The observance of Ash Wednesday is now entirely religious, a day when many people start to deny themselves some small thing for the whole of Lent and when, in Roman Catholic churches, the ashes of the palms used on the previous Palm Sunday are blessed. At the service the congregation kneel to have their foreheads marked with ash in memory of the fact that all men are dust and must to dust return. The old custom of throwing at a puppet called Jack-o-Lent on Ash Wednesday has now quite died out; it lasted longest in Cornwall, where a straw figure in old clothes was carried through the streets and afterwards hanged with a good deal of rough merriment. It was supposed to represent Judas Iscariot, but more probably it originally stood for the dying Winter.

Sundays were exempted from the general Lenten fast but no real festival followed until Mothering Sunday, the fourth in Lent, when children away from home returned to visit their parents, and servants were given a special holiday for the same purpose. They took with them presents for their mothers, the most usual being a bunch of flowers and a simnel cake. These cakes are still made in enormous numbers in Devizes and Bury at this season, and are sent all over the world. In both towns baking begins immediately after Christmas to allow time for the cakes to reach people living abroad. Many emigrants to the Dominions left standing orders fifty or sixty years ago for simnels to be sent to them, and these orders have been renewed by their children and grandchildren. There are two kinds of simnels, one very rich and rather like a bride-cake, with a ring of almond paste on top, and the famous Bury simnel, which is flat and made with currants, candied peel and spices.

At Chilbolton in Hampshire Mid-Lent wafers take the place of simnel cakes. It is not known when this custom first started, but from the nature of the wafers themselves it is clear that it was in pre-Reformation times. They have been made by one family, the Baverstocks, for at least two hundred years; the secret recipe is carefully handed down from mother to daughter-in-law in each generation, and is never given to anyone outside the family. The wafer-irons used are known to be three hundred years old and are kept in Winchester Museum during the year, being temporarily returned to Chilbolton for use shortly before Mothering Sunday. They are formed of two round iron plates pivoted on long handles. The plates are heated in a wood fire and the batter is poured on the lower one when it is hot and pressed into shape by the upper. There is a local tradition that these wafers were once made at a nearby monastery and were given to the congregation after Holy Communion as a memento on Mothering Sunday, when all those who usually worshipped at chapels-of-ease made a special journey to attend service at the Mother Church of the parish.

In north-eastern England peas or beans fried in butter with vinegar and pepper are still served in many houses on Passion or Carling Sunday. There is considerable doubt as to the meaning of the word "carling"; in the Midlands the day is called Care Sunday, a name which is supposed to refer to the sorrow or care of Our Lord's Passion, which now begins to be foreshadowed in the church ceremonies. On Palm Sunday almost everywhere branches of willow or imported palm are carried in the churches and crosses of palm are often distributed to the congregation in memory of Our Lord's entry into Jerusalem. On this day also an ancient pagan custom is, or was until a few years ago, kept up by the children of Bradwell and Castleton. They drop straight new pins into certain wells of the district and into a pond between Bradwell and Brough. They say that if they do not the Lady of the Well will not let them have clean water and, which probably matters more to them, their Easter Monday bottles will break. These are glass bottles filled with water in which pink peppermint cakes of a particular shape are shaken until the water is sweet enough to drink. The belief in well and water spirits was general for centuries after the introduction of Christianity, and is responsible for many of our existing superstitions and ghost stories, but it is not often that it is so clearly stated in modern times as by the children of these two upland villages.

England is one of the few European countries where the ancient and once general custom of Royal Maundy gifts is still kept up (28–30). On Maundy Thursday purses of money

32, 33 Children's Seasonal Games: Hopscotch and Whipping-top

From eighteenth-century engravings

34, 35 Children's Seasonal Games: Marbles and Peg-top

From eighteenth-century engravings

are given in Westminster Abbey to as many poor men and poor women of London as there are years in the reigning king's age. Until 1689 the king came in person and washed the feet of the poor people before the distribution, in memory of Our Lord's similar service to His Apostles on that day. James II was the last to perform the ceremony in its entirety, and after his time the first part of the service was omitted: the Maundy Money was still given, but by proxy. To-day the Archbishop of Canterbury, as Lord High Almoner, distributes the purses, except very occasionally, when the king comes himself. In 1932 King George V made his gifts in person, and so also did Edward VIII in 1936.

The ceremony now consists of prayers, psalms and a lesson, followed by the distribution of red and white purses which are brought in on a great dish by the Yeomen of the Guard (28). At one time food and clothing were given; when Queen Elisabeth "made her Maunds" in 1572 she gave to each person enough broadcloth for a gown, a pair of sleeves, half a side of salmon, ling, six red herrings, bread and claret. Queen Victoria in 1838 gave woollen and linen clothing, shoes and stockings to the men, and 35s. to the women instead of clothes. To-day money is given in place of both these doles, and this, in red purses, forms the first part of the distribution. While they are making it, the Archbishop and the Dean of Westminster wear only plain white instead of the gorgeous robes in which they began the service, and carry linen towels on their shoulders to commemorate the lost custom of washing the feet. Afterwards the white purses are distributed. These contain the real Maundy money, specially minted silver pennies and twopenny, threepenny and fourpenny pieces to the value of one penny for each year of the King's age. These coins, which have not altered since the time of Charles II, are still legal tender, though they are usually kept by the recipients as souvenirs of a great occasion.

Hot-cross buns are eaten throughout England on Good Friday, though as a rule they are no longer made at home. These little cakes have a long history, and seem to be descended from the wheaten cakes eaten at the Spring Festival alike by Greeks, Romans and Saxons. It is still believed in country districts that bread and buns baked on Good Friday never go mouldy and can be used as cures for various ailments. It was formerly the custom to keep at least one from each year's batch, not only for possible medicinal use but also as a protection against fire. In a London public house, *The Widow's Son*, a fresh bun is annually placed in a basket containing its predecessors (31) by a sailor who is given free beer as a reward. A clause in the lease enforces this custom, which is said to have been started by a widow who refused to give up hope when her sailor son failed to return from one of his voyages, and continued to set aside a bun for him every year. The collection now (1941) totals one hundred and seventy-one buns which, during air-raids, are taken to a place of safety along with the other valuables of the house.

Children in many districts make a point of playing marbles on Good Friday, and at Brighton during last century the whole fishing community used to skip on what was locally known as Long Rope Day. The regular seasonal appearance of certain children's games is very curious (32–35). Any motorist will have noticed the rhythmic regularity with which spinning-tops appear on the hard surfaces of the roads in the early part of the year. Every village and town is full of them for a time and then they are seen no more. So, too, with skipping, hop-scotch, marbles and other games; they begin in their due season according to some unknown rule, are played everywhere for a while and then end as mysteriously as they began.

There is an old tradition that the Crucifixion took place on March 25th, and consequently it is thought to be unlucky if Easter, the day of resurrection, falls on Lady Day. An old rhyme says:

> If Our Lord falls in Our Lady's lap
> England will meet with a great mishap.

Another version of the superstition says this refers to Good Friday itself, and that some national misfortune will follow if it coincides with its supposed original date. Those who cling to this belief point to the fact that it happened in 1910 and King Edward VII died after a short illness in the following May.

There are some anniversaries which usually fall in Lent but are not of it. St. David's Day on March 1st is celebrated by all Welshmen by the wearing of leeks or daffodils. It is usually said that the leek became the emblem of Wales because it commemorates the battle of Hatfield Moor in A.D. 653, when the Britons under Cadwalla defeated Edwin of Northumbria. According to legend, they wore leeks in their hats, acting on the advice of St. David. If they did, it was probably because the plant already had some symbolical meaning for them; certainly St. David could not have given his advice at the time, for had he lived until then he would have been more than two hundred years old. He is supposed to have lived for several years on bread and wild leeks alone, and this may have helped to sanctify the plant in the eyes of his followers. The old custom of *Cymhortha*, when farmers met to help each other, included a communal meal to which all brought their share of leeks, nothing else being used to make the soup on this occasion. At Jesus College, Oxford, where there are always a large number of Welsh students, leeks are worn on St. David's Day, and this is also the custom amongst officers and men of the Welsh regiments (39). The daffodil is associated with St. David because it is traditionally said to bloom first on his day. It is an easier emblem to wear than the older leek, and every schoolchild in Wales sports one, real or artificial, on March 1st.

Shamrock is worn by all Irishmen and by many who are not Irish on St. Patrick's Day, March 17th. St. Patrick is supposed to have used the plant as an illustration of the doctrine of the Trinity when he was preaching to the pagan Irish. It was an example they could readily understand, for shamrock was already sacred to them because its leaves formed a triad. It was also believed that snakes were never seen near it, and it thus became easily associated with the legend that St. Patrick drove all the reptiles out of Ireland.

One of the most charming ceremonies in London is the Oranges and Lemons service at St. Clement Danes. It takes place every year on March 31st or as near as possible to that date, and is a modified revival of an old custom which has only recently died out. In the lifetime of many elderly people now living, the attendants of Clements Inn used annually to visit all the residents of the Inn and present them with oranges and lemons, receiving some small gift in return. At the March service, the church is decorated with oranges and lemons, and all the children who attend are given fruit as they leave the building (36), while the bells play the old nursery rhyme. The oranges and lemons are supplied by the Danish colony in London, whose church this has been for many centuries, and are often distributed by Danish children wearing their national colours of red and white. When the famous bells were re-hung

6

in 1919 they too were decorated with oranges and lemons (27), and were re-dedicated in the presence of Queen Alexandra, once herself a princess of Denmark. It is sad to think that the bells were destroyed when the church was hit in an air-raid in 1941, when they had been brought to the ground floor of the tower on their way to a place of safety.

36 St. Clement Danes. Oranges and lemons distribution

From a drawing by A. Forestier

37 Hocktide at Hungerford. The scene in the Court

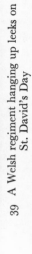

39 A Welsh regiment hanging up leeks on
St. David's Day

38 Hocktide at Hungerford. A tutti-man taking
toll of kisses

Chapter V

EASTER

THE festival of Easter is named after the Saxon goddess, Eostre, in whose honour, as Bede tells us, the month of April was once called Eosturmonath.[1] She seems to have been a spring or dawn goddess, and as was natural at that time of the year, her feast took the form of a spring celebration. The date of the Christian Easter was settled in A.D. 525 to be the Sunday following the first full moon after the Vernal Equinox, or March 21st; if the first moon happens to be full on a Sunday, Easter Day is held on the Sunday after. Thus it can never be earlier than March 22nd or later than April 25th, and must always fall in that lovely season when spring is really beginning and when, in spite of our erratic climate, and its occasional late frosts and snowfalls, every day shows some fresh and heartening sign of the summer to come.

Churches throughout Christendom are decorated with flowers for this festival of hope fulfilled. The author of *The Festival*, published in 1511, tells us that

"This day is called in many places, Godde's Sondaye; ye know well that it is the maner at this daye to do the fyre out of the hall, and the blacke winter brandes, and all thynges that is foule with fume and smoke shall be done awaye, and there the fyre was shall be gayly arrayed with fayre floures, and strewed with grene rysshes all aboute."

Because of the change in the Calendar which made everything eleven days earlier, we cannot now so confidently put out our fires for Easter Sunday, and our spring-cleaning is consequently somewhat later in the year, but it is still the custom for most women to wear some new garment for the morning service. It used to be considered unlucky to do otherwise; in northern England it was said that crows would befoul old clothes if anyone was rash enough to appear in them on that day.

On Easter Eve in Roman Catholic churches new fire is made

[1] Bede, *De Temporum Ratione.*

6*

47

by striking flint against steel, and with the flame so obtained the Paschal candle is lit. This was formerly the custom in the English Church also. In the churchwardens' accounts at Reading we read that 5s. 8d. was spent in 1559 "for makynge of the Paschall and Funte Taper," and two years earlier an Easter candle weighing three hundred pounds was set up in Westminster Abbey. The method of making the fire is interesting because it marks a change-over from an earlier custom. The sacred and purifying character of new, or need, fire is a very ancient belief, and formerly most ceremonial bonfires were lit from it. The old way was to kindle the flame by the friction of wood against wood, the spark being caught by dry chips placed in the hollow where the spindle was turned. While this was being done, all household fires had to be put out, or the flame would not come; later they were relit from the new fire. As late as the beginning of the present century, the Midsummer bonfires were lighted in this way at Studfold Ring in Yorkshire. The Church forbade the use of wood as a pagan survival, and in its own services substituted the more modern flint and steel. Now this later method is itself out-of-date, but it is still adhered to in the Roman Catholic service on Holy Saturday.

An egg is an obvious symbol of resurrection and new life, and has been so regarded in many religions beside our own. It is a natural gift for Eastertide, both because of its symbolism and because it was then once more possible to eat eggs after the Lenten fast. In mediaeval times they were blessed in the churches, and the form of prayer sanctioned by Pope Paul V definitely associates them with the Resurrection. It runs:

"Bless, O Lord, we beseech Thee, this Thy creature of eggs, that it may become a wholesome sustenance to Thy faithful servants, eating in thankfulness to Thee, on account of the Resurrection of our Lord."

Our modern Easter eggs of chocolate or pasteboard are a development of the old pace-egg, which was simply a hard-boiled egg with the shell dyed red or green or yellow. The household accounts of Edward I for 1290 include an item of four hundred and fifty eggs to be coloured and distributed at Easter, for which the sum of eighteenpence was paid. Even allowing for the great difference in the value of money then, this is a figure to rouse bitter envy in the hearts of housewives to-day. In Cheshire the children still go "pace-egging" on Easter Monday, though little is now left of the old custom except a rather threatening little rhyme which promises the ungenerous that "your hens shall all lay addled eggs and your cocks lay stones." In Lancashire the Pace-Egging Play was formerly given at this time with the full paraphernalia of blackened faces and animal skins. The old game of Egg-rolling is still kept up at Preston, where large crowds assemble to watch the coloured eggs being rolled down a grassy slope in the Park. It is also played at Barton-on-Humber, where the eggs are rolled along a lane until all the shells are broken. At Birkenhead some grassy mounds called the Bouks were used, the object of the players being to pass the eggs unbroken through wickets at the foot of the slope. The Bouks are now part of a rather dull municipal Park, and the startlingly rapid growth of what in 1816 was described as a small village "nine miles north-north-west of Great Neston" has swept away the traditional game, along with almost every other relic of the town's rural beginnings.

The round biscuit-like "Easter cakes" which are sold in most confectioners' shops at this season are the descendants of the spiced cakes once generally eaten then. Until recently in the West of England the clerk of each parish used to visit all the principal houses and present every member of the family with a cake. In Kent a kind of cheese-cake locally known as a "pudding-pie" was specially baked. Tansy cakes or puddings were played for on Easter Wednesday in many districts. They were made from tansy and other herbs and were eaten with the meat course at dinner, perhaps as a survival of the time when eggs and green herbs formed the principal Easter dish. At Twickenham two large cakes were once brought to the church and divided amongst all the young people present at the Sunday service. In 1645 Parliament forbade this pleasant custom as a "superstitious practice" and ordered that bread should be given to the poor instead. For many years this distribution was made by throwing penny loaves from the top of the church steeple to be scrambled for by an expectant crowd of poor children assembled in the churchyard below. A similar scramble for bread thrown from the steeple formerly took place at Paddington on the same day.

Until 1864 University College, Oxford, preserved a curious

49

custom known as Chipping the Block, the origin and meaning of which seems to be now forgotten. On Easter Sunday a long pole was decorated with greenery and set up outside the Hall. The cook and his assistant in their white caps and jackets stood on either side of it holding pewter dishes, one of which was empty while the second contained a blunt chopping-axe. As the Master and Fellows came out, they took the axe and struck the pole, and then put money for the cook in the empty dish. An old tradition said that if anyone who had dined in Hall could cut the pole in half with one blow, he could lay claim to all the estates of the College. This was denied by those in authority but, in any case, the question was purely academic, since it would have been physically impossible for anyone, however strong, to sever the pole at a blow with the axe provided.

At Hallaton in Leicestershire the annual Hare-pie Scramble and Bottle-Kicking is held on Easter Monday (40, 41). This custom is very old and its date of origin is unknown. It is connected with a piece of land said to have been left at some remote date to the Rectors of the parish on condition that they provide every year two hare-pies, two dozen penny loaves and a sufficiency of ale, the pies to be scrambled for at Easter on a piece of rising ground known as Hare-pie Bank. It is, of course, not possible to have hare-pie at Easter as hares are not then in season, so beef-steak is used instead. The pies are made in the Rectory kitchen and are first divided amongst some hundreds of people on the lawn, after which the remainder is put into a sack and carried in procession to Hare-pie Bank. Here the pieces are thrown to the crowd and scrambled for with great vigour.

With the procession go three men carrying the "bottles" for the Kicking. These are in reality three small barrels painted in bright colours and decorated with ribbons; two contain beer and the third is a dummy. The procession circles the village, gaining fresh adherents all the way until the bank is reached. After the pie-scramble is over, one of the full barrels is put into a circular hollow on the top of the bank and the game begins. There are two sides, the Hallaton men and the "Medbourne" men, who include not only people from that parish but also those from any other nearby village who care to join in. These try to get the barrel away from the local team by kicking it over the Medbourne boundary; the defenders for their part try to kick it over the brook which is their own boundary line. Whoever wins claims the ale. Then the dummy barrel is fought for and finally the third is broached on the village green and drunk with full ceremonial honours, the leader of the winning side being hoisted on to the old Cross and given the first drink amid much cheering.

Hares have always been traditionally associated with the Easter festival. In France the children are told that they go to Rome in Holy Week to fetch home the Easter eggs; in some parts of Germany they are said to lay them, and children are sent to search for a hare's nest. At Coleshill in Warwickshire it was formerly the custom for young men to catch a live hare before ten o'clock in the morning on Easter Day and present it to the clergyman, who was bound to give them in return a calf's head and a hundred eggs for their breakfast and a groat. In Leicester the Mayor and Corporation in their scarlet robes used to go to Black Annis' Bower on the Dane Hills every Easter Monday to "hunt the hare." Originally, no doubt, this was a real hunt; in later times instead of the traditional quarry a dead cat soaked in aniseed water was dragged over the ground in front of the hounds. At Hallaton the image of a sitting hare was sometimes carried on the top of a pole during the procession to the bank. This is rarely done now, but the rest of the rite is carried out as vigorously and enthusiastically as ever. In the eighteenth century an attempt was made to abolish it by a rector who considered the money for the pies and ale might be more usefully spent in some other way. The villagers retorted by chalking "No pie, no parson, and a job for the glazier" all over his walls and doors. The clergyman took the hint and prudently abandoned his reforming efforts.

The Bottle-Kicking is possibly older than the Hare-pie scramble with which it is associated, and may be a survival of the symbolic driving away of winter which often formed part of rural spring ceremonies. In the Isle of Man a fight between the followers of the May Queen and the Winter King took place on May-day, in which the latter were always defeated and their leader chased over the parish boundaries. At Neston in Cheshire a man mounted on a donkey used to ride through the village on Easter Monday and was pelted with mud and rotten eggs all the way. He was given a sum of money for this performance, which was known as Riding the Lord, and certainly he earned it.

51

At Ashton-under-Lyne Riding the Black Lad took place on
Easter Monday, and was supposed to perpetuate the hated
memory of Sir Ralph Assheton who in Henry VI's time
tyrannised over the local people. According to the local
tradition, he was Lord of the Manor of Middleton and inherited from his father the right of riding round certain lands
in Ashton parish, and fining or otherwise punishing the tenants
who neglected them and allowed *carr-gulds*, or weeds, to
flourish on them. This he did with great severity once a year,
and these annual inspections, coupled with other tyrannies,
earned him the lasting hatred of the people. His son abolished
the custom after his death, but for some unexplained reason he
perpetuated the memory of his father's misdeeds by leaving
money to pay for an annual procession on Easter Monday in
which a Black Knight was the principal figure.

Such is the extremely improbable legend which is locally
given as the reason for the custom. Whether Sir Ralph really
was the tyrant of popular belief it is now difficult to say; he
seems to have made a deep impression on the people of his day,
and possibly there was some reason for it. In the rental of
Sir John de Assheton for 1422 it is stated that he and his two
sons, Rauf and Robyn, "have the sour carr guld rode and
stane rynges for the term of their lives," so the weed inspections
may actually have taken place. If Sir Ralph carried out this
duty too rigorously or with too high a hand, he may well have
made himself greatly disliked and feared. But if every hated
overlord was thus remembered we should have Black Knight
processions in more places than Ashton-under-Lyne. It seems
more probable that his name was attached to a figure which
already typified something universally execrated and that he
became associated with the annual custom of driving out the
Winter. An effigy in black armour, such as he was supposed
to wear on his rides, was set on horseback and paraded round
the town. At one time the initials, or some emblem of the
occupation, of the first couple to be linked together during the
year were emblazoned on the armour, supposedly in commemoration of the fact that Sir Ralph was the child of a second
marriage. At the close of the procession the figure was taken
to an open space and there shot to pieces with guns, stones
and any other handy missiles amid the delighted jeers of the
people. This custom was kept up every year until 1938, and
was made the basis of an elaborate pageant organised by the

traders of the town some six years ago. It seems a pity that a traditional custom which has survived for so many centuries should now be allowed to lapse, and it is to be hoped that it will be revived again before long.

At Thaxted Easter Monday is celebrated by Morris dancing in the streets and by country dances in which anyone who will may join. This is now one of the earliest Morris performances to be given in the year; the old dance at Christmas has disappeared from most villages, and Whitsuntide or May-day is the usual beginning date for Morris teams.

Hocktide falls on the Monday and Tuesday after Easter Week and is observed with much ceremony at Hungerford on the second day. This interesting old town is still governed, not by a Mayor and Corporation but by an elected Constable, Portreeve and Bailiff, and a Court of Feoffees consisting of twelve elected citizens who deal with fishing and common rights and similar matters (37). John of Gaunt granted certain manorial rights to the town and presented the people with a horn which is still kept in the Town Hall. Formerly it was used at Hocktide, but in 1634 a new horn was made and inscribed with the words

"John a Gaun did give and grant the riall of fishing to Hungerford toune from Eldren stub to Irish Stil except some several mil pound"

and this is now blown at the opening of the ceremonies on Hock Tuesday.

Up till recently a watercress supper consisting of black broth, welsh rarebit, macaroni, watercress salad and punch was eaten on the Monday night, but this now seems to have lapsed. At eight o'clock on Tuesday morning the Town Crier sounds the horn on the balcony of the Corn Exchange, and the bellman starts on his round of the streets, crying

"Oyez! Oyez! Oyez! All ye commoners of the Borough and Manor of Hungerford are requested to attend your Court House at the Hall at nine o'clock this morning to answer your name on penalty of being fined. God save the King."

The two elected Tutti- or tything-men go down to the Constable's house to fetch the tutti-poles, long staves decorated with ribbons and having a nosegay and an orange on the top. At nine o'clock they go off to visit the commoners' houses, and at the same time the Court of Feoffeement meets to elect the new Constable and officers and to hear claims for fishing and common rights. This session is followed by a civic lunch, the newly-elected Constable presiding with the two Tutti-men seated on either side of him. After the meal, guests and new commoners have to submit to the time-honoured ceremony of "Shoeing the Colt." The Chairman remarks that there are strangers present, and at once two men enter, one wearing a blacksmith's apron and carrying a hammer, and the other carrying a box of farrier's nails. The foot of the first stranger is seized by the "blacksmith," who pretends to drive nails into the sole of his shoe with strong blows until the "colt" has had enough and purchases his freedom by treating the company to a round of drinks. Anyone who refuses to be shod is fined one pound, but of course no one ever does refuse, and the shoeing goes on until all the newcomers are accounted for.

The most interesting part of Hock Day is undoubtedly the parade of the Tutti-men. These, accompanied by the Orange Scrambler who carries a sack of oranges and wears cocks' feathers in his hat, visit every common-right house in the town and demand from every man a coin and from every woman a kiss (38). If the kiss is given, an orange is exchanged for it, and the tutti-poles have to be constantly replenished from the Orange Scrambler's sack. Not only the commoners' womenfolk but every woman met with, whether a resident or merely a passing motorist, has to meet the traditional demand, or pay a fine of one penny. After the lunch already mentioned, the remainder of the oranges are thrown to a large crowd of of children who have assembled for the purpose, most of whom have been eagerly following the Tutti-men about all the morning.

The origin of Hocktide is obscure. In some ancient leases rents were paid then and at Michaelmas, and the season itself was one of festivity. It seems to have been the custom from an early date for men and women to take it in turns to collect money for the needs of the parish church, the men on Monday and the women on Tuesday in most places, but sometimes the other way round. Peshall, quoting from the records of St. Mary's Church, Oxford, tells us that in 1510 the churchwardens received "of the wyfes gaderynge, XVs ijd," and in the accounts

40 The rival captains brandishing the 'bottles' before
the contest

41 The Rector of Hallaton cutting the hare-pie at
the start

THE HALLATON BOTTLE-KICKING AND HARE-PIE SCRAMBLE, LEICESTERSHIRE

42 Choirboys beating the bounds at St. Giles Cripplegate, London

for St. Mary-at-Hill, London, in 1496 there is an item, "Spent on the wyves that gadyred money on Hob Monday, 10d." In 1499 St. Lawrence's Church at Reading received 20s. from the women and 4s. from the men. It is interesting to observe that in almost all the records extant the women are shown as better collectors than the men. The favourite method of extracting money was to stretch a rope across the road and to refuse to allow anyone passage without payment of a small fee. Possibly on the men's day, the women were allowed to give a kiss instead of money, and this may account for the poor results already mentioned.

Hocktide celebrations declined after the Reformation, though we read of collections thus made for St. Peter's-in-the-East at Oxford as late as 1667. But at least a part, and that perhaps the oldest, of the custom persisted for many years, not on the original two days but on Easter Monday and Tuesday. "Lifting" was practised in Cheshire up to the end of last century. On the Monday the young men carried round a decorated chair and lifted the women in the houses they visited, receiving a kiss or money in return. On the Tuesday the women did the same thing for the men. At Neston the chair was omitted, and the girls were supposed to bar their doors when they saw the young men approaching. If, however, a window was left open, it was regarded as an invitation to enter and lift the women, notwithstanding their feigned reluctance.

Lifting was not always so politely carried out as in Cheshire, where it survived longer than in most other places. In industrial towns shy members of the public were liable to be unceremoniously hoisted by bands of brawny men or women and roundly kissed whether they consented or not. Baring-Gould relates that a school inspector of his acquaintance once rashly visited Warrington on Easter Monday and was seized by a party of girls and carried round the town in spite of his protests. A similar fate overtook another man in Wednesbury who "was lifted and kissed till he was black in the face by a party of leather-breeched coalpit women."[1] In north-east England girls had their shoes pulled off on Monday and boys lost either their shoes or their caps on the following day. It seems probable that the church collections at Hocktide were simply adaptations of a much older agricultural rite associated

[1] W. Henderson : *The Folklore of the Northern Counties of England.* Footnote by S. Baring–Gould, pp. 64–5.

with spring, and that the ancient part of the custom persisted after its connection with the Church had been forgotten. Lifting at Easter prevailed in other countries also, and Baring-Gould mentions that he was himself lifted by a party of Basque women when travelling one year in the Pyrenees.

A word may perhaps be said here about England's patron saint since his day, April 23rd, must fall somewhere near all but the earliest Easter. St. George has not the intimate personal connection with England that St. David and St. Patrick have with Wales and Ireland, and perhaps for this reason he has not made so deep a mark on English folk-custom. He is said to have appeared to Richard I. and his army before Acre during the Crusades, and long before he was adopted as the official patron of this country, he was a very popular saint here. He was the original hero of the Mumming play before he became confused with the kings of his name who reigned over us in Hanoverian times, and he still remains the type of Christian chivalry for most of us. His cross is the symbol at once of England, as apart from Great Britain, and of the Church of England, and his flag is usually flown on all great Church festivals. The Knights of the Order of St. Michael and St. George meet in St. Paul's Cathedral on April 23rd to commemorate their dead and welcome new members, and on this occasion they wear long mantles of brilliant blue lined with scarlet. When men wore more colourful clothes than now, it was customary to wear a blue coat on St. George's Day, and this may have been done in imitation of the blue cloaks of the Order. Many people to-day wear red roses in his honour, and if the national flower of England is not as much in evidence as are leeks or shamrocks in March, the difficulty of procuring roses in April is perhaps enough to explain this apparent neglect on our part.

Chapter VI

ASCENSION AND WHITSUNTIDE

B EATING the Bounds takes place in many parishes during
Rogation Week, and often includes an open-air service in the
fields. In ancient Rome the *Terminalia* marked the feast of
Terminus, the god of fields and landmarks, and the *Ambarvalia*
on the Ides of May included the sacrifice of animals for the
benefit of the crops, and processions round the fields. From
these two celebrations our Beating the Bounds seems to have
sprung. Mamertus, Bishop of Vienne, appointed litanies to be
read during the perambulations of parishes in the fifth century,
and Rogation processions were definitely established as part
of the Church's ritual at the Council of Orleans in 511. In
Saxon times Rogation-tide was known as the Ganging Days,
because the people went about the parish then for the blessing
of crops. At the same time, the boundaries were marked, an
important matter when maps were few and inaccurate and
hardly anyone could read. The children especially had the
boundary marks impressed on their young minds by being
soundly bumped or whipped at every important point. They
were thrown into ponds or rivers, forced to climb over the
roofs of houses that straddled the line, rolled into briar hedges,
or bumped on boundary stones; in after years, if any dispute
arose, they had the most painful reasons for remembering what
was or was not the actual boundary at any given point. After
it was all over they were solaced with presents of money or
cakes or willow wands. This part of the ceremony persisted
in many places after the field service had died out, and to-day
children still take part in the procession with long wands in
their hands, with which they beat the marks (42) instead of
being themselves beaten, as in the past.

In Elisabeth's reign the clergy were enjoined to admonish
the people at certain points along the route and to pronounce
a solemn curse on anyone who moved or altered the boundary
mark. The Gospel was read at various prominent stones or
trees on the line, and wells were blessed during the procession
as well as the fields. In *The Country Parson*, published in 1652,

7

Herbert says that every clergyman ought to encourage his parishioners to take part in the rite for four reasons:

"First, a blessing of God for the fruits of the fields.
2. Justice in the preservation of bounds.
3. Charitie, in loving walking and neighbourly accompanying one another, with reconciling of differences at that time, if there be any.
4. Mercie, in relieving the poor by a liberal distribution and largess, which at that time is or ought to be used. Wherefore he exacts of all to be present at the Perambulation, and those that withdraw and sever themselves from it he mislikes, and reproves as uncharitable and unneighbourly; and if they will not reform, presents them."

The tracing of the boundary line often involves a long and circuitous journey, especially in towns where buildings have been set up without respect for parish limits. In St. Clement Danes parish the line runs down the Thames at one place, and the clergy and choristers have to take to boats to cover it. Twenty-five of the old marks of this parish still survive, all with the anchor of St. Clement on them. In the Savoy Liberty the procession has to penetrate into the Temple and into the vaults of a bank in search of its marks. At Bodmin the course runs for several miles across country. The ceremony here takes place only at long intervals and has not preserved much trace of its religious origin. At various points hurling is played, and at Saltings Pool, the last mark on the line, the Mayor throws the ball into the water and a wild scramble ensues. Whoever rescues it receives ten shillings, and a further fifteen shillings is paid to the man who succeeds in holding it against all comers and carrying it back to the Mayor. He has to be a fast runner and particularly skilful in dodging his opponents, for one of the few rules in this contest demands that if any other player touches him, he must release the ball at once.

In Oxford some boundary lines run through College grounds, and it is a pleasant sight on a fine morning to see the choristers of St. Mary's Church in their blue cassocks thrashing a mark in the inner quad of All Souls, or scrambling for the halfpennies thrown to them by the Fellows. After the bounds of St. Michael-in-the-Northgate have been beaten, a lunch is held in the Hall of Lincoln College, at which a curious concoction

43 The Bampton Morris dancers performing in the street

44 Scrambling for hot pennies, Lincoln College, Oxford

46 The green garland cross, Charlton-on-Otmoor, *ca.* 1800

45 A dressed well, Tissington, Derbyshire

known as ground ivy ale is served. Here, too, there is a scramble for the children, this time for hot pennies (44). When in 1940 Lincoln College was not available because the Government had taken it over, the lunch was held in a snack-bar in Market Street, where the floor of one room has a stone in it marking the boundary of the parishes of St. Michael and St. Martin.

At Helston a clod of earth and a slip of hawthorn are placed on every mark and beaten by the boys. At Lichfield the cathedral clergy and choir carry elm boughs during the procession, and a passage from the Gospels is read at eight places where wells formerly existed. After the perambulation, a blessing is given by the font in the Cathedral, and here the elm branches are left. In the Tower of London the bounds are beaten every three years, the next occasion being in 1942. The Yeoman Warders take part in the procession, the Chief Warder leading with the Tower mace, and the Yeoman Gaoler bringing up the rear with an axe over his shoulder. The perambulation of St. Mary's parish, Leicester, is also triennial, and here, where any house stands on the boundary line, the front and back doors are left open to admit the procession. It was formerly the custom in this parish to set any newly appointed official head downwards in a hole on a certain bank, and to beat him with a shovel whilst in that undignified position. Even the clergy were not exempt, and on one occasion a new curate had to suffer the ordeal. In some places the Mayor or Council officers used to be ducked or bumped by way of impressing the extent of their jurisdiction upon them, but generally these physical reminders were confined to the children, as having more impressionable memories and less dignity to lose.

The fields are blessed at Twyford during the beating of the bounds there, and at Cannington in Somerset, though there is no formal perambulation, the clergy and children visit all the fields and allotments during Rogation week, carrying with them wands on to which bunches of flowers are tied. A short service is held in one of the fields, and then the procession returns to the Church, singing a litany. At North Shields an open-air service is held on the fish quay and the nets and trawlers are blessed, after which the clergy go in a launch to bless the boats in the harbour and then sail up the Tyne, which forms the boundary between North and South Shields for a certain distance. At Cullercoats they sail into the harbour to bless the boats, and at Hastings, St. Leonards and Mudeford, near Christchurch, the sea, the boats and the nets are all blessed during waterside services held for the purpose.

Abbotsbury Garland Day may perhaps be mentioned here, for, though it has no connection with beating the bounds, it was formerly associated with the opening of the fishing season. This custom, which is undoubtedly very old, and bears traces of pagan sacrifice to the sea, is now only a shadow of its former self; with the decline of the fishing industry, it has lost much of its meaning, since the garlands cannot now be used for their original purpose. On May 13th the children make garlands of a traditional shape, which are carried on a stick and the flowers for which are carefully collected for some days beforehand. With these they visit the houses of the village and are given money, which they share out at the close of the day. The garlands themselves are often left at the War Memorial in the churchyard. Formerly they were taken to church at noon for a children's service, and were then placed on the bows of the fishing boats. The afternoon was kept as a general holiday, with dancing and games on the green below the Castle and on the beach. In the evening the boats put out to sea for a short distance and the garlands were thrown into the water "with a prayer," according to some accounts, "with a song," according to others. The words of the song used seem to have been lost. One old lady now aged ninety-three remembers a boat named *Rabbit*, the crew of which always had a rabbit's head in their wreath. With the throwing in of the garlands and the return of the boats the fishing season was considered to be formally opened, and the ceremony was annually performed till there were no boats left to take part in it. All that now remains is the rather meaningless, though charming, custom still kept up by the children on the traditional date.

Well-dressing at Ascension-tide survives in several places in Derbyshire, Staffordshire and Gloucestershire. At Tissington and Buxton the wells are "dressed" with large framed panels consisting of elaborate and often very ambitious pictures of Biblical subjects, beautifully executed by local craftsmen who have been doing this highly skilled work for years (45). The surface of the panel is spread with smooth clay dampened by salt water, and on this groundwork are pressed leaves, flower petals, berries, moss and bark. Fir-cones, larch-buds, mosses and leaves provide the light and dark greens, minute petals of wallflowers, lilac, aubretia, rock-roses, bluebells and other flowers are used for the delicate colours of the faces, hair and dresses of the figures, grains of rice and sago, grey lichens and oatmeal make the clouds and shadows. Different subjects are chosen every year, and the damp clay keeps the finished picture fresh and glowing for several days. The panels are set up above the wells very early in the morning; later in the day clergy and people go in procession to all the wells to bless them and return thanks for the gift of water. At Buxton the whole town is decorated with flags and greenery for the occasion, the Mayor and Corporation take part in the procession, and after the wells are blessed a Festival Queen is crowned by the Mayoress. At Endon the two wells are dressed on May 29th, and the May Queen is crowned on that day, a pleasant blending of ancient well-worship, May-day rites and Restoration rejoicings.

The Tissington ceremony is said to have been held first in 1350 in thanksgiving for the people's escape from the Black Death. Although nearly half the inhabitants of Derbyshire died from this terrible plague, Tissington was untouched, and this immunity is usually ascribed to the purity of the water in its five wells. Probably it helped to keep the people healthy, as the remoteness of the village helped to protect it from travellers who might have brought infection, but it may be doubted whether this was the true reason for the well-dressing custom. Wells are dressed in other places which have no such legend of safety, such as Belper, Wirksworth, Baslow and Bisley, to name only a few. It is possible that a new meaning was given to an ancient rite in Tissington by the peril so providentially averted, and an added reason thus found for continuing or reviving it. There is a tradition that the ceremony was omitted once in Puritan times, and the springs immediately dried up, and this rather significant story is also told of the brine well in Droitwich. Aubrey says:

"This custome is yearly observed at Droitwich, in Worcestershire, where on the day of St. Richard, they keepe holyday, and dresse the well with green boughs and flowers. One yeare in the Presbyterian time it was discontinued in the civil warres, and after that, the spring shranke up or dried up for some time; so afterwards they revived their annual custom, notwithstanding the power of the parliament and soldiers, and the salt water returned again, and still continues."

A curious custom is kept up every Ascension Eve on the sands at Boyes Staith, Whitby. This is the building of the Penny Hedge, a stout fence of stakes and interlaced boughs which is set up at the water's edge early in the morning and has to be strong enough to withstand three tides. The word "penny" is a corruption of penance. According to the local legend, some twelfth-century hunters of noble family killed a cleric, either by accident or from anger at his refusal to admit them during an hour of prayer. The Abbot of Whitby ordered them to build a hedge every year on the shore, while the Town Crier read an account of their crime and sounded a blast on a horn. The first hedge was set up in 1160. Since that time the custom has been modified, so that it is no longer the descendants of the murderers who do the work, and the recital of the crime is omitted. But the hedge is still built in the old place, and at the end of the ceremony the bailiff of the Manor sounds his horn and cries "Owte upon they!" as his predecessors have done for over seven hundred years.

Whitsun has always been a time of festivity. It was one of the seasons at which Miracle Plays were acted, when the Church sought to teach the truths of religion to an unlettered people by simple and easily understood dramas. In Chester such plays were regularly acted from 1268 to 1574, and were not finally abandoned for some time after the latter date. The twenty-four Guilds of the City were each responsible for one scene, and the whole sequence covered the story of salvation from the Creation of the world to the Last Judgment. The scenes were acted on double-decked carts which were drawn about the town, the actors dressing in the lower portion and performing in the upper. In Coventry similar plays were given at Corpus Christi.

A simpler festivity was the Whitsun Ale, when a King and Queen were chosen and Morris dancing, games and sports were held. The money collected at this time went to the upkeep of the parish church and the relief of the poor. In the Introduction to Aubrey's *Survey and Natural History of the North Division of the County of Wiltshire* we read:

47 Garland crosses on the screen, Charlton-on-Otmoor, Oxfordshire, 1822

48 The trial at the Dunmow flitch celebration: a candidate-couple under cross-examination

49 Service conducted from the open-air pulpit in the first quadrangle, Magdalen College, Oxford, on St. John the Baptist's Day

50 The Minehead hobby-horse by the Yarn market, Dunster

"There were no rates for the poor in my grandfather's days: but for Kingston St. Michael (no small parish) the Church-Ale of Whitsuntide did the business. In every parish there is (or was) a church-house, to which belonged spits, crocks, etc., utensils for dressing provision. Here the housekeepers met and were merry, and gave their charity. The young people were there too and had dancing, bowling, shooting at butts, etc., the ancients sitting gravely by and looking on. All things were civil and without scandal."

In 1574 the lease of a certain house in Whitwell, Isle of Wight, was granted to John Brode on condition that the rooms could be used at any time for a Church-Ale "for the maintenance of the chapel." In many parishes the Churchwardens' accounts include items paid out for the Whitsun Ales, or received from them, as at St. Lawrence's Church in Reading, where we read that 22s. 6d. was collected by the "maydens" in 1505, and 23s. 4d. was paid out in 1557 for the "Morrys Daunsers and the Minstrelles, mete and drink at Whytsontide."

The election of a King and Queen survived at Downham, near Clitheroe, until about the middle of last century. The prettiest girl in the village was chosen as Queen by a committee of young men; presumably the girls chose the King. The crowns used were of iron, and they and the wearers were decorated with flowers. The King and Queen headed the procession to Downham Hall, followed by their attendants and javelin men, and there led the dancing and games. The holiday lasted for two days, and was ended by the ceremonial drinking of "the Queen's Possett," towards the cost of which everyone contributed a shilling.

In later years the village clubs inherited many of the old Whitsun Ale customs in their annual Club Feasts, which usually took place at Whitsun or a little later. The principal celebrations on these days was a church service, followed by a procession, Morris dancing and games. Not many of these rural clubs now survive, but a few still carry on good work and provide an annual holiday for their members. At Marnhull in Dorset the Club meets every year on the last Wednesday in May, when all the members go in procession to church and afterwards parade round the village, wearing rosettes and carrying banners. The day ends with a dinner, and games and sports on the Recreation Field. At South Harting in Sussex, the Club members plant beech boughs on Whit Monday and carry carved hazel rods at the church service. The Sick Club at Stoke Abbott has its annual "walk" on the first Friday in June, the programme being much the same as at Marnhull. Similar processions can still be seen in a number of villages in northern England.

In Manchester and Salford the town holidays fall in Whit Week, and the two annual Walking Days are held on Monday and Friday. These two days are the great event of the year for thousands of schoolchildren who take part in the procession. On Monday the Church of England and Nonconformist scholars parade the town, on Friday the Catholics have their procession. All traffic is held up, the shops are closed, and spectators come in from all the surrounding districts. Each school vies with its fellows to produce the finest spectacle. Money is saved up all the year round, even in the poorest homes, to dress the children in white frocks and suits, shoes and stockings, and to provide the veils and wreaths, the bouquets of flowers and other things required. The processions take three and a half hours to pass a given point, and are a charming sight, with their banners and flower-wreathed statues, and the thousands of white-clad children with serious, happy faces. Grown-up people also take part, and there are some who have never missed walking in the annual procession for fifty or sixty years. The children cover a prescribed route round the two cities on the two principal days, and then each parish has its own procession on the following Sunday. "Walking Day" is found all over Lancashire and Yorkshire, and nearly every town and village has its parade, in some places at Whitsun and in others on the patronal festival of the church.

The Dunmow Flitch is still awarded on Whit Monday to those who are brave enough to claim it and can prove their case. It is given to married couples who have never quarrelled or wished themselves single again since their wedding. The custom is supposed to have been started in Henry III's reign by Robert Fitzwalter, who arranged for a flitch of bacon to be given to any man who could swear before the Prior and villagers of Little Dunmow that he had never repented of his marriage, waking or sleeping, for a year and a day. He had to kneel on two sharp stones in the churchyard to take the oath, and was afterwards carried through the streets in a chair which is still kept in the church. The first recorded award was to Robert Wright in 1445, but the custom is mentioned by Chaucer a hundred years earlier as being well known in his time. Before the Reformation the inquiry must have been very searching, for we only hear of two other prize-winners, Stephen Samual in 1468 and Thomas Ley in 1510.

The wife's views on the marriage were not consulted until the beginning of the eighteenth century. In 1701 John and Ann Reynolds and William and Jane Parsley received gammons, the first couple for ten and the second for three years of unruffled married harmony. The custom has been abolished several times by different Lords of the Manor. It was stopped in 1752 and although it was revived again, it was never afterwards held in Little Dunmow. It was once more abolished in 1809, but after the publication of Harrison Ainsworth's *The Flitch of Bacon* it was re-instituted and held at Great Dunmow, and now seems firmly established. It is held sometimes at Ilford (48), sometimes at Saffron Walden, sometimes at Great Dunmow. The claims are tried before a jury of six spinsters and six bachelors; the trial is conducted with a great deal of hilarity and is a Bank Holiday parody of Divorce Court proceedings. In spite of this, there are nearly always some genuine candidates for the flitch, as well as those who only take part for amusement, and two flitches are given, one for sincere claimants, and a second which is divided so that all who have the courage to come forward and face the chaff and fun of the court may have something for their pains. A similar award was once given at Wychmore in Staffordshire, but this seems to have died out completely and to have been claimed only very occasionally while it lasted.

At Bampton in Oxfordshire the Morris dancers go round the houses on Whit Monday and dance on the lawns and in the street (43). There are two teams here, one of which claims a continuous history of over five hundred years. The members are dressed in white, with flowered and ribboned hats, ribbons fluttering on their clothes, and brightly coloured bell-pads on their legs. Only six dance at a time, the other two standing out until their turn comes. There is also a Fool with a bladder on a stick, a fiddler, and an interesting character known as the Sword-bearer, who carries a large cake impaled on his sword. At one period in the day the two teams join forces for a united and extremely effective display in the Market Place. The almost equally famous Headington troupe also dance on Whit

Monday, as well as on May-day after the carol singing on Magdalen Tower. It was this team which Cecil Sharp first saw dancing at Christmas in the grounds of Headington Hall, near Oxford. They came with many apologies for performing at what they considered to be the wrong season but "times were hard," and they hoped to gain a little extra money by this additional performance. This discovery of a still living dance interested Cecil Sharp in folk dances as well as songs, and in this way helped to promote the movement to preserve and revive these ancient ritual dances all over England.

51 The College Choir singing Latin hymns on the top of Magdalen Tower, Oxford, at 6 a.m. on May-day

52   The Chimney-sweeps' Jack o' the Green, in the eighteenth century, London

Chapter VII

MAY-DAY

MAY-DAY is a festival of purely pagan origin, a simple and spontaneous expression of joy at the beginning of true summer. In the Church's calendar it is the feast of St. Philip and St. James, but these saints have little connection with the traditional ceremonies, every one of which is a celebration of welcome to the long warm days and short nights to come, the return of vegetation and flowers, and all the compensations that summer brings to a northern country. The garlands still carried by the children, the maypole itself, at once the symbol of the flowering tree and of fertility, the old bonfires, the carols sung on towers and high places, and the now almost forgotten custom of spending the night in the woods and bringing back green branches in the morning, were all intended to mark the return of summer. It was because the Puritans, nearer in time and thought to their primitive origins than we are now, recognised many of these customs for the fertility rites that they actually were, that they hated them so bitterly and put them down wherever they could; and it was precisely because they were rooted in the deepest and most primitive instinct of humanity that all the sermons, Acts of Parliament and legal repressions of the seventeenth century failed to suppress the time-honoured ceremonies or eradicate them from the hearts of the people. To-day we celebrate May-day eleven days earlier than before the change of the calendar, and often have to shiver in consequence while we carry out the rites more appropriate to the warmer May 12th, or Old May Day. But an erratic climate has bred in us a fine disregard of weather, and we continue to welcome summer with maypoles and garlands and a host of old customs, the meaning of which are often quite unknown to the participants, but which always have been carried out at this season, and it is to be hoped always will be.

Not all the old May ceremonies have survived. Until the middle of last century May Eve was marked by the visits of the May Birchers, who came round to the different houses of the parish and decorated the doors with boughs of trees or flowers by which they expressed their opinion of the occupants. In Cheshire the plants chosen were supposed to rhyme with the word that best described those who lived within. The fair in face or character had pear boughs set over their doors, the glum had plum branches, the morose had alder, locally pronounced "owler," which rhymed with scowler. A thorn branch meant an object of scorn, and gorse in bloom over a woman's door conveyed the worst of insults. In Hertfordshire the unpopular might find their thresholds disfigured by nettles or some other unpleasant weed. This custom caused a great deal of ill-feeling, and it is not surprising that in these milder and less outspoken days it has been abandoned. In the Isle of Man children went round, and sometimes still do, with little posies of flowers which were laid on the doorstep or fastened to the post, and rowan crosses made without the use of a knife were tied to the tails of cattle. This last was a precaution against witches, who were supposed to meet on May 1st and to have great power at this season.

In Lancashire and Cheshire the May-singers went about during the last few evenings of April singing their traditional song. In one Cheshire version the master, mistress, daughters and sons of the house are all mentioned in turn, with particular good wishes suited to their age and circumstances, and the last verse runs:

> So now we're going to leave you in peace and plenty here,
> For the summer springs so fresh, green and gay;
> And we'll come no more a-Maysinging until another year,
> For to drive the cold winter away.

Near Burnley April 30th was known as Mischief Night, when shopkeepers' signs were changed, gates were taken off their hinges and hidden, and all sorts of practical jokes were played, until the custom finally became unbearable for the quieter citizens, and was stopped by the police.

Those who went a-Maying sometimes started out at midnight or earlier and spent the whole night out of doors; sometimes they set off in companies just before dawn and were ready to greet the first light with drums and blasts upon cowhorns and other instruments. In times of moral laxity this custom did, without doubt, lead occasionally to scandals, but often it was innocent enough. At Eton the boys were allowed to rise at four in the morning and gather branches with which to decorate the school windows; according to an old MS. in the British Museum, this was permitted only "if they can do it without wetting their feet." Stow tells us how Henry VIII

". . . on May Day in the morning with Queen Katharine his wife, accompanied by many lords and ladies, rode a-Maying from Greenwich to the high ground of Shooter's Hill; where, as they passed by the way, they espied a company of tall yeomen, clothed all in green, with green hoods and with bows and arrows, to the number of two hundred. One, being the chieftain, was called Robin Hood, who required the king and all his company to stay and see his men shoot."

Girls collected May-morning dew in which to wash their faces, as this was supposed to be an infallible beauty-charm. The *Morning Post* for May 2nd, 1791, notes that

"Yesterday being the 1st of May, according to annual and superstitious custom, a number of persons went into the fields and bathed their faces with dew on the grass, under the idea that it would render them beautiful."

In Suffolk the servant who was the first to bring in a branch of hawthorn in full blossom was given a dish of cream, a custom which died a natural death after the calendar change in 1752, since the hawthorn which is usually in flower by May 12th blooms only rarely in time for the new May-day.

For the same reason May garlands no longer contain the white and red flowers which were always formerly included. These garlands were so important a part of the May ceremonies that the day was often called Garland Day, and they are still to be seen in a number of districts. They vary considerably in shape and form; sometimes a long chain of flowers is used, sometimes a simple posy is tied to the top of a long wand. Occasionally a cushion of flowers is made, or crossed hoops are covered with blossoms and greenery. In Oxford little boys parade the streets with crosses of leaves, bluebells, and, oddly enough, since these are carefully omitted in most places, cuckoo-flowers. At Flore, near Weedon, the school-children make an elaborate floral crown which is carried on two long poles by the senior boys and is taken round to the houses of the village before the coronation of the May Queen.

At Cowley St. John, now part of Oxford, there is a flower service in the church, to which all the children bring posies. In the same county, at Charlton-on-Otmoor, a clipped yew cross hangs throughout the year on the rood-screen (46, 47), and on May-day it is decorated with flowers. The children also make small wooden crosses covered with flowers, which they carry round the village, singing a carol outside each house. Formerly the ceremony was more elaborate. A large garland was made every year and was carried about by two men who were accompanied by Morris dancers. At the end of the day the garland was taken to the church and hung on the rood-screen, where it was left until the time for dressing it came round once more. In 1857 the procession and dancing were abolished, but the re-decoration of the yew cross in the church and the making of smaller crosses by the children still takes place every May-day.

In Southampton an early morning service is held on the top of Bargate, and at Oxford a similar ceremony takes place on Magdalen College Tower (51). The origin of these customs is a little obscure. It has been suggested that the Oxford ceremony sprang from a Requiem Mass once said on the tower for Henry VII, which was changed after the Reformation to the present service. But a tower is a curious place for the singing of Mass, and the choice of such a venue as this and the top of a high gate at Southampton suggests an origin much more remote. The use of high places for ritual acts is very ancient, and both these May-day customs may have sprung from some memory of primitive worship on hills and towers. A curious custom connected with a hill persisted in Horncastle until the beginning of last century. The boys of the town went to the top of a hill called May Bank early in the morning, and from there walked in procession to the maypole at the other end of the town, carrying white willow wands wreathed with cowslips. Arrived at the may-pole, they all shouted and struck their wands together, and then scattered the flowers over the ground. The wands were known as May-gads. Only boys took part in the rite, and the procession always started from the same hill-top, which may have been a sacred place in pagan times.

In Oxford the choristers of Magdalen Choir School assemble on the tower at six o'clock and sing *Te Deum Patrem colimus* and other Latin hymns (51), while a large and silent crowd stands

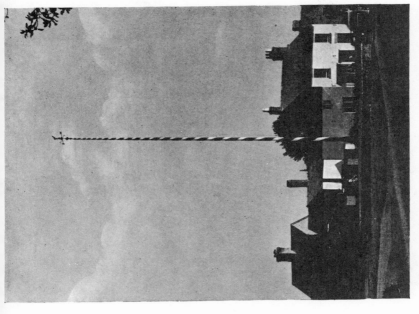

54 The Maypole at Welford-on-Avon, Warwickshire

53 The Maypole, Barwick-in-Elmet, Yorkshire

56 The Carthorse Parade, Regent's Park

55 Blowing the May horns, Heamoor, near Penzance

on the Bridge below to hear them and the chorus of birds in the surrounding trees singing together. At the end of the service the bells are rung, and then the Headington Morris team dances in the streets, first at Milham Ford, and then in Radcliffe Square and Broad Street, and finally by the Martyrs' Memorial, after which they and the spectators return home to a much appreciated breakfast. Formerly there was a Chimney Sweeps' procession also, with a Jack-in-the-Green (cf. 52) and a Lord and Lady, but this has now disappeared. It was also a great day for College "rags" of the noisier type, and in 1940 the ghost of the old spirit raised its head, first in the sudden appearance of a number of undergraduates in surplices who gave a burlesque rendering of *Ilka' Moor* on the Bridge before the service, and later in the day in a free fight between a political procession and undergraduates of a different opinion, which continued nearly all the way to the meeting-place in St. Giles, and ended with a loud and competitive singing of rival political songs in which both parties did their best to drown the voices of the other. Many people were mildly shocked by both these demonstrations but, in fact, they were quite in keeping with the old "May sports" and "Mischief Nights" which once, at least in towns, often made May 1st as boisterous and turbulent as it was in other respects beautiful and interesting.

The May Queen has survived in almost every place where May-day celebrations are held, but the King has disappeared almost completely. He was formerly quite as important as she was, and we have already seen how the Twelfth Night and Whitsun ceremonies both included a King as well as a Queen, the former being the more important of the two at Twelfth Night. The Oxford Lord and Lady just mentioned were in the same tradition. They were not crowned, but were dressed in gay be-ribboned clothes and walked in the procession immediately behind the garland, holding a white handkerchief between them by its two ends. The Queens now are usually children but formerly they were young girls chosen for their beauty and popularity, and their crowns were covered with flowers and leaves brought in at dawn with the rest of the greenery collected by the Mayers.

Most villages now have their elected May Queen, and so do the majority of London schools. In some parts of the North the coronation takes place, not on May-day but during the

Wakes, and the child is then usually known as the Rose Queen. A modern extension of this old idea is the annual election in Lancashire and Cheshire of a Cotton, Silk and Dairy Queen. The choice of the Cotton Queen is a matter of interest for local newspaper readers for some weeks beforehand, the candidates being pretty mill-girls whose photographs appear in rotation and are voted for by the readers. The Queen, when elected, is an important personage, who is expected to visit the various cotton towns and take part in all sorts of civic functions, dressed in her velvet robes and crown, which must often be very hot and uncomfortable on blazing summer days. In the intervals of these royal progresses, she works in the mill as usual. The Silk and Dairy Queens have the same duties, and all three are said to do a great deal of good work for their respective trades during their term of office.

In London each school elects its own Queen, and on the Saturday nearest May 1st a May Queen of London is chosen and crowned on Hayes Common, near Bromley. After the coronation she receives the homage of all the lesser school-queens. This, of course, is a modern ceremony, but it is carried out with all the zest and vigour of the older village rites, at least as far as the children taking part are concerned.

Knutsford's Royal May Day is not held on May 1st, but on some convenient date either in May or June. It is a civic function of some importance and includes all the time-honoured features, the long procession through the streets, with the Queen and her maids of honour, sword-bearer and attendants of both sexes, Morris dancers, Jack-in-the-Green, Robin Hood and Maid Marian, and the town's famous sedan chair, followed by the coronation on the Heath, maypole dancing, sports and games. It attracts thousands of visitors every year and, though perhaps a little artificial and over-organised now, it is a charming spectacle in the narrow streets of the old town, and on the wide and open Heath surrounded by its dignified Georgian houses.

Maypoles are still the central feature in most village cele-brations. These gay, tall shafts, with their flowers and ribbons, representing a living tree and the principle of fertility, were objects of particular hatred to the Puritans, who connected them directly with paganism. Stubbes, in his *Anatomie of Abuses*, describes with dislike the bringing in of the "Maie poole" in his day. He says:

72

"They have twentie or fourtie yoke of oxen, every oxe havying a sweete nosegaie of flowers tyed on the tippe of his hornes, and these oxen drawe home this Maie poole (this stinckying idoll rather), which is covered all over with flowers and hearbes, bounde rounde aboute with stringes, from the top to the bottome, and sometyme painted with variable colours, with twoo or three hundred men, women and children followying it with greate devotion. And thus being reared up, with handkerchiefes and flagges streamyng on the toppe, they strawe the grounde aboute, binde greene boughes about it, sett up sommer haules, bowers, and arbours, hard by it. And then fall they to banquet and feast, to leape and daunce about it, as the Heathen people did at the dedication of their idolles, whereof this is a perfect patterne, or rather the thyng itself."

The earliest maypoles were not permanent shafts, but were young trees brought in from the woods, as Stubbes describes. In Cornwall a tall elm was fetched home on April 30th, painted and decorated, and set up in the middle of the village. In some parts of Wales a birch tree was similarly treated. In Herefordshire the word maypole was applied to a birch which was decorated with red and white streamers and was set up outside the stable on May-day as a protection against witches for the rest of the year. The permanent maypoles were often immensely tall, like that set up in the Strand in 1661, which was 134 feet high. Seamen had to be brought from the docks with pulleys and anchors to raise it. St. Andrew Undershaft in Leadenhall Street takes its name from the maypole which used to be set up in front of the south door and which was taller than the church itself. Stow tells it was never used after the "evil May-day" of 1517, when the apprentices, jealous of the alien traders in the city, started a riot in the course of which the maypole was pulled down. Until 1552 the pole hung in Shaft Alley, being "laid along over the doors and under the eves of one row of houses." In that year a curate of St. Katharine's Church denounced it as an idol and prevailed upon the people to cut it up, each householder taking the piece which hung over his own door for firewood. Another maypole suffered eclipse at Rostherne in Cheshire, but not as the result of a preacher's eloquence. The Vicar, Adam Martindale, had indeed preached against it, but the villagers, less inflammable than London folk, remained unmoved. Mrs. Martindale, therefore, took the law into her own hands. Going out at night with three of her maids, she cut it down with their help, leaving only a short stump which she said would serve as a "diall-post."

At Barwick-in-Elmet, near Leeds, there is an eighty-foot maypole (53) which is taken down every three years to be repainted and have its garlands renewed. The next occasion will be in 1943. The pole is taken down on Easter Monday and set up again on Whit Tuesday, when all the traditional May festivities are held, even though not on the traditional date. The arrangements are in the hands of three elected Pole Men; the four garlands are made by the local Girl Guides, and consist of a wire foundation about eighteen inches high which is covered with rosettes, brighty coloured ribbons and artificial flowers. At Temple Sowerby the Lord of the Manor has to replace the maypole on the village green whenever this becomes necessary. At Welford in Warwickshire there is a very tall pole which is painted with red spiral stripes (54), and standing poles can also be seen at Wellow, Preston Brockenhurst, Donnington and some other places. At Shipston-on-Stour a temporary maypole is set up in the middle of the main street, and round it the children dance to the music of a fiddle, regardless of motorists and other travellers who are thus held up and made to contemplate for a short time the living past in the present. Torrington has two maypoles at once, set side by side in the square, and the double dance, with its white-clad children threading their way through the intricate figures and the two sets of moving coloured ribbons, is a very lovely sight indeed.

At Appleton Thorn in Cheshire the old ceremony of Bawming the Thorn is carried out, not on May-day but early in July. Here the children, after a procession, dance round a living tree, an ancient thorn from which the hamlet takes its name and which is popularly supposed to have sprung from a cutting of the Holy Thorn of Glastonbury. It is now protected by iron railings, and these and the branches are decorated with garlands of flowers and ribbons for the occasion. The word "bawming" is an old dialect word which is said by some authorities to mean "adorning" and by others to mean "anointing." The custom is interesting both because it is a rare survival of dancing round a growing tree instead of a temporary branch specially brought in or the later maypole shaft, and because it perpetuates in some degree the old reverence for single trees in a central position which were often regarded as "guardian" trees, and under which, in early times, councils were held and justice administered. In the middle of last century the celebration was allowed to lapse because it was supposed to lead to rowdiness and damage to property, but it was revived again in 1930 and has been carried on ever since.

The principal performer in Padstow's May-day celebrations is the Hobby-Horse, a man entirely hidden in an enormous covered hoop surmounted by a grotesque head and a long pointed cap. With him go a number of men with blackened faces and one dressed in woman's clothes. The proceedings begin at midnight on April 30th, when the Horse and his attendants start off on their rounds, singing

> Unite, unite and let us all unite,
> For summer is a-coming to-day,
> And whither we are going we will all unite,
> In the merry month of May.

They stop outside each house and sing as many verses of the song as there are occupants within, each person being called by name and wished happiness; one verse refers to "Aunt Ursula Birdwood," a mysterious character like the "Aunt Mary Moses" of the Helston Furry Song. The Hobby-Horse dances in the roadway, with caperings and prancings, and finally suffers a ritual death very realistically portrayed. This goes on until every house has been visited, and then there is a lull until eight o'clock, when the second procession begins. This time the house-to-house visits are accompanied by a demand for money. There are a number of other parades during the day, in one of which the Hobby-Horse is made to drink from the Traitor's Pool and the spectators are sprinkled with water. The dance, with its sacrificial death, goes on all the time, and the whole town is gaily decorated for the occasion. There is a local tradition that this custom commemorates the discomfiture of some French troops who landed in the bay, mistook the red cloaks of mummers for soldiers, and fled, but of course the custom, with its luck-bringing visits, its dying Horse and its sprinklings of water over the people, is very much older than the eighteenth century, when this mythical event was supposed to have taken place.

Further up the coast, at Minehead, there is another hobby-horse parade on May-day. The "horse" in this case is really a ship. The hoops are covered with brightly coloured cloth of a cheerful design which reaches to the ground and hides even the feet of the performer (50). The top is made of cardboard in the form of a ship and covered with hundreds of coloured paper strips, with a mast and sails made in the same way in the centre. A cow's tail is fastened to the stern, and this is used to belabour anyone rash enough to refuse a gift to the toll-gathers who form part of the procession. The celebration here is somewhat quieter than that at Padstow, and is rather less interesting. There are no early morning visits and traditional chorus, and the ship-man does not so much as dance as glide through the streets, going through a few ambling steps outside each house on the route. The hobby-horse is said to have acquired its ship-form and its cow's tail after a storm on April 30th, 1722, when a ship was lost with all hands off Dunster, and a dead cow was washed ashore from the wreck.

May-dolls are still carried round with or without the garland in Ilfracombe, Bishop's Teignton and Edlesborough. They are usually ordinary feminine dressed dolls, and were supposed to represent the Blessed Virgin, whose month May is. Probably at one time they had another meaning also, and were connected with the May Queen and the summer. At Polebrooke formerly two were carried in the procession in a bower of flowers and greenery immediately behind the Queen. At Edlesborough there are also two, one doll having a smaller one in her lap, and these are said to represent the Virgin and Child. They are taken round in a decorated chair, which is sometimes covered by a white sheet. This is removed while the children sing a carol welcoming the summer, giving the impression that in uncovering the dolls they are revealing the incarnate summer to the listeners. At Bishop's Teignton one or two dolls are carried about in a flower-filled cradle by the little girls of the parish. The boys here carry short, flower-wreathed poles, which are sometimes expanded into a fan shape. In an interesting letter to *The Times* of May 10th, 1927, the Rev. M. McIntyre says that one such pole had a doll attached to it, which he believed was meant to represent the almost vanished May King. He adds:

"The children have no idea of any meaning attaching to

57 Rushes on the nave floor of St. Mary Redcliffe, Bristol, Whit Sunday

58 The Rush-bearing procession at Ambleside, 150 years ago

From a contemporary engraving

their action; but expectation is written on their faces and pennies are expected by each child. The children call it the May-Day Doll. So far as I can see it is not etiquette to come out on the quest for pennies after 12 years of age for a girl or 14 for a boy."

Cart-horse parades are a great feature of May-day in London (56) and Manchester, when the great animals appear in all the glory of their horse-brasses, ribbons and rosettes. Some of these brasses are very old and have been in the owner's family for generations. They were originally intended to serve not as ornaments but as amulets to protect the horse and its driver against witchcraft and evil, and even modern ones are usually cast in the traditional shapes—crescents, single or triple, stars, hearts and wheels. The older sets are often extremely heavy and are only brought out for these parades or other important occasions. In coaching days the mail-coaches were decorated with lilac and laurel boughs on May 1st and travelled thus throughout the day; even the slower and more cumbersome road-waggons had their share of gaiety, for we read in the *Gentleman's Magazine* for 1754 that passengers used to give the waggoner a ribbon for his team at every inn on the way until "the poor beasts were almost blinded by the tawdry, party-coloured flowing honours of their heads."

One other May custom may be mentioned here, if such a name can be given to that which does not occur. It is still very generally considered unlucky to be married in May, and for this reason many brides will either hurry on their weddings so that they may be celebrated in April, or wait until June. This belief about a month which began with a fertility festival seems curious, and may have come down to us from the Romans, who shared it. For them May was a time of purification; on the 9th the *Lemuralia*, or Feast of the Dead, was held, when sacrifices were made to purge each house of hostile ghosts. The women's festival of *Bona Dea*, at which no man might be present, also fell in May, and the season was considered unpropitious for weddings exactly as it is now. The Catholic dedication of the month to Our Lady may also have helped to associate it with chastity and virginity, and so have strengthened the old superstition, which is certainly as strong to-day as it ever was.

Chapter VIII

SUMMER AND AUTUMN

LITTLE now remains of the great Midsummer festival which our ancestors celebrated with so much rejoicing. The bonfires that once starred the hills everywhere on Midsummer Eve are only a memory in most places, though they are still lit with due ceremony at St. Ives in Cornwall, Penzance and Lands End, and at Whalton in Northumberland. In the last-named place the people keep to the older calendar and dance round their huge bonfire on July 4th, Old Midsummer Eve. The ancient pagan festival of the Summer Solstice fell on June 21st; it was superseded in Christian times by the Feast of the Nativity of St. John the Baptist, three days later, but the change made little difference to the rites held at that season. The great bonfires, once lit in honour of the sun, were transferred to St. John's Eve and burnt as brightly as ever until the middle of last century; if the primitive sacrifices of men and animals were forgotten, young people still leapt through the flames for luck, and cattle were driven over the dying embers as a protection against the murrain. Sometimes, indeed, the old rite was carried out in full. Even as late as 1800 one Cornish farmer sacrificed his best calf in the flames, and Robert Hunt tells us that when he was correcting the proofs of *Drolls, Tradition sand Superstitions of Old Cornwall* in 1865 he heard of a similar case which had occurred only a few years earlier at Pontreath. The ashes of the bonfires were strewn over the fields to bring fertility to the crops, and men went about the farms and villages with blazing torches for the same purpose. Girls practised charms to discover their future husbands, and fern-seed was sought for on Midsummer Eve as a means of making the finder invisible.

The Christian saint was easily connected with the fire festival in people's minds, both because his bones were traditionally said to have been burnt by the Emperor Julian and because he himself said that, as Christ must increase, so must he, the forerunner, decrease, a statement readily illustrated by the fact that his feast fell on the longest day, after which the sun's power would decrease until the Winter Solstice.

Stow tells us that in London fires were lit in the streets, every householder contributing his share of wood and labour, and lamps burnt all night over the decorated doors of the houses. "Some," he says, "hung out branches of iron, curiously wrought, containing hundreds of lamps lighted at once." In Burford a dragon and a giant were paraded through the village. The local explanation of this custom was that it commemorated a victory won by Cuthbert, King of the West Saxons, whose standard was a golden dragon; but the connection of dragons with fire is too well known for any further explanation to be necessary for a custom associated with a sun festival.

Houses everywhere were decorated with fennel, orpine and St. John's Wort, and in Cornwall the long poles that marked the boundaries of the tin mines were crowned with flowers. Bishop Pocock[1] relates how the men of "the countree uplond" brought flowers and branches to London so that the citizens might "make her houses gay into remembraunce of Seint Johan Baptist, and of this it was prophecied of him that many schulden joie of his burthe." Such decorations at a time of festivity were traditional and hardly need explanation, but they were usually supposed to be in memory of St. John's life and preaching in the wilderness. At Magdalen College, Oxford, an annual sermon is preached on Midsummer Day from a stone canopied pulpit in the wall of the first quadrangle (49), and formerly the sides of the quadrangle were fenced with green boughs for the occasion. This sermon, which was discontinued for many years and revived in 1896, commemorates the fact that there was once a Hospital of St. John the Baptist on this site, the buildings of which were granted by Henry VI in 1457 to William of Waynflete, the founder of the college.

A curious and interesting ceremony of uncertain age takes place at Stonehenge on June 21st or 22nd. A modern order of druids holds a service round the Altar Stone at dawn, walking first in procession round the circle in their white robes and scarlet hoods, and saluting the sun as it rises. This order, which is known as the Church of the Universal Bond, claims to be a survival of the ancient druids of Britain. Its members say that the druids were never entirely suppressed, and although persecuted and driven underground, existed either openly or as

[1] Quoted by J. Brand, *Popular Antiquities*, Vol. 1.

a secret society from pre-Roman times to the present day. They claim to have records of their own formation dating from the fourteenth century and to preserve a list of the Chief Druids for the past five hundred years. They believe also that the ancient druidic rites did not include human sacrifice, as is usually supposed, and that, in worshipping God the All-Father rather than the sun, they are carrying on the old faith. It seems extremely doubtful whether this rather ambitious claim to antiquity could be substantiated. There is little or no trace of an active body of druids after early Saxon times, and though the priests of the British Church were sometimes called by that name, they were definitely Christians and cannot have had any real connection with the older religion, however much they may have differed from Rome on such matters as the marriage of the clergy and the date of Easter. Whether a secret order of druids did persist longer than is usually thought we cannot say with certainty, but it seems hardly likely that they can have carried on their rites for long without the knowledge of the powerful mediaeval Church. However this may be, the Order exists now, and celebrates the Summer Solstice by a service which, if not in direct continuity with the ancient sun-worship rites, is at least held in the same place and at the same hour as those Midsummer ceremonies which are believed to have taken place at Stonehenge in primitive times.

The lovely custom of rush-bearing can still be seen in many parishes during the summer, though it is now only a survival of what was once a useful and necessary act. Before the introduction of boarded floors in churches, the aisles were strewn with rushes, and these were ceremonially renewed every year at the patronal festival. The procession of the rush-cart was the great event of the day. Every hamlet attached to the church-town contributed its quota, and the great pile of rushes was placed in a decorated harvest wain and secured with flower-covered ropes and harvest gearing. Occasionally a bower of oak-boughs was built on top of the towering mass, in which sat a man who directed the proceedings. Girls and children carrying garlands walked beside the cart and in front went the Morris team, dancing the Long Morris processional as the wain moved along and the Cross Morris at every big house or other customary stopping-place. As the procession approached the church, the bells were pealed, and then the sweet-smelling reeds were taken down and strewn thickly over

59 Rush-bearing procession at Ambleside. Note tall rush pillars and floral harp

60 A Harvest home supper in a barn at Burderop Farm, Swindon, Wiltshire

61 Harvest-home rejoicings on a farm 150 years ago

From a contemporary coloured engraving

the earthen floor of the building. Often the graves were strewn with rushes also, and this is till done in July at Tarvin in Cheshire and a few other places.

The introduction of floor-boards made rushes no longer necessary for warmth and dryness, and no doubt the insanitary habit of leaving the old rushes to be covered by the new fresh green carpet which existed in some parishes helped in the gradual decline of the custom. It has not, however, entirely died out yet. The great cart is now seldom, if ever, seen, but rushes and hay are still laid in many churches. At Barrowden in Rutlandshire the reeds are brought in on St. Peter's Eve and left on the floor for a week. Grass is strewn at Shenington on Trinity Sunday and the Sunday following, and new-mown hay is laid down at Glenfield on the Thursday after July 6th, the old village feast-day. At Wingrave, near Aylesbury, hay is brought in on the Sunday following St. Peter's Day from a field bequeathed to the parish by a woman who once lost her way at night and was saved by the sound of the church bells. The revenues of this field are used not only to provide the hay but also the more modern floor-coverings in the form of carpets and hassocks.

At Warcop and Great Musgrove in Westmorland the actual rush-bearing has died out, though in the former parish the choirboys carry rushes on St. Peter's Day, a custom introduced by the Vicar a few years ago to remind the people of the true meaning of the anniversary. In these villages the day is marked by the girls who come to church wearing light wooden crowns entirely covered with flowers, crowns which were originally worn for the now abandoned rush ceremony. Another charming addition to the old custom survives at St. Mary Redcliffe, Bristol, where bouquets of flowers are placed in every seat of the church. In 1493 William Spensor, once mayor of the town, left money for an annual sermon to be preached before succeeding mayors on Whitsunday at the time of the rush-bearing. To-day the aisles are strewn with rushes as in his time (57), and the Lord Mayor takes part in a procession to the church, where he is met by the Bishop of Bristol and ushered in to the sound of trumpets to hear the sermon arranged for by his fifteenth-century predecessor.

The most famous rush ceremony is that at Grasmere, which takes place on the Saturday nearest to St. Oswald's Day, August 5th, and which has never been allowed to lapse, though it has been held on other dates at different times. The clergy head a procession round the village in which walk six girls carrying a sheet full of rushes, and villagers with their "rush-bearings." These are rushes skilfully made up into traditional patterns, such as the crown or hand of St. Oswald, harps and maypoles, serpents on poles, helmets, carriages, wishing-gates, the child Moses in a basket, and many other complicated designs (58, 59). The procession moves round to the sound of St. Oswald's Hymn and the Rushbearing March, and then enters the church, where a sermon is preached and the rush-bearings are laid on shelves round the building or hung on the walls. In 1940 there were 173 rushbearings, most of them made in the forms handed down from one generation to another. At the end of the service the children are given a piece of gingerbread stamped with the name of St. Oswald. The rushbearings are left in the church till Monday, when they are fetched away by their owners, and a procession sets out for the School Field, in which sports and tea are held. Formerly the men had wrestling matches on this day, but this is now confined to the village boys.

London children can sometimes be seen on July 25th with little grottoes made of oyster shells which they set up on the pavements or carry about with the reiterated request, "Please to remember the grotto." They do this, though they do not know it, in honour of St. James the Great, whose feast-day it is. In the Middle Ages those who made the pilgrimage to the saint's shrine at Compostella were entitled to wear a scallop-shell as a badge, and it was believed that those who had the right to wear it would be remembered on the Day of Judgment. A curious legend connects the Apostle with these shells. He was beheaded in A.D. 44, and the story goes that his headless body was placed in a marble ship which miraculously floated to Compostella. As it neared the coast of Portugal, a wedding was being held at Bonzas. The bridegroom's horse bolted with him and plunged into the sea but, the ship passing over them, horse and rider were saved by the power of the saint. As they emerged from the water, the man's cloak was seen to be thickly covered with shells, and from that time the scallop-shell became one of the emblems of St. James. Oysters come into season on Old St. James's Day, and superstitious people believed that whoever ate them then would not lack for money during the rest of the year.

Formerly the orchards were blessed on July 25th. In some districts St. Peter and St. Swithun are also associated with apples, and in Herefordshire it used to be said that unless they were christened on St. Peter's Day, the crop would be poor. St. Swithun is thought to be baptising the fruit if a shower falls on July 15th, and the old superstition still lingers, in spite of frequent evidence to the contrary, that if it rains then it will rain for forty days afterwards. St. Swithun was Bishop of Winchester in the ninth century and, according to tradition, desired to be buried, not in the Cathedral but outside, where the rain might fall upon him. This was done, but nine years afterwards plans were made to give him what was considered more honourable burial inside the building. Rain fell in such torrents on July 15th, the day appointed for the translation, and for forty days thereafter, that the project had to be abandoned, and from this legend arose the belief that the saint had the power to influence the weather at this season.

In June the householders of Ock Street, Abingdon, elect the Morris dancers' Mayor, a custom which lapsed for fifty years and was revived in 1938. A wooden box is placed on a table in a sidestreet, and into it the people drop their voting-cards, which are counted in the open air before the candidates. Afterwards the newly elected Mayor is "danced in" up and down Ock Street, and during the following days there are further performances in various parts of the town and a supper to finish the proceedings. The custom is said to have begun in 1700, but it may be a relic of an older practise. In many places mock mayors used to be elected during fairs and at the patronal festival, regardless of the existence or otherwise of a real mayor. In Cornwall Ovingham Fair on October 25th was followed by "Gwonny Jokesane's Day," when a mayor was chosen and carried about in a disorderly procession. Who or what Gwonny Jokesane was is not known. At Penryn the journeymen tailors chose the wittiest man among them to serve as their mayor on "Nutting day," which fell when the hazel nuts were ripe. The election took place in the neighbouring parish of Mylor and the selected candidate was called the Mayor of Mylor. He was carried on the shoulders of four men into Penryn, preceded by torch-bearers and a band; bonfires were lit in his honour and there was a display of fireworks at night. At Leigh in Lancashire one of the townsmen was annually elected Lord Mayor for a day, and similar customs were kept up in Staffordshire and Flintshire. Unlike the Ock Street election, which is a serious choice of the Morris leader, most of these ceremonies degenerated into simple burlesques before they died out altogether. Their origin is obscure. In some places vague and unsubstantiated traditions of lost charter rights existed, but generally those who took part could give no better reason than old established custom. G. L. Gomme[1] suggests that the true origin may perhaps be found in the simultaneous existence in remote time of tribes of differing stock in the same place, and that the mock mayor may be a memory of the chosen leader of the weaker of the two communities. It is noteworthy in this connection that the mock mayor at Penryn was chosen outside the town boundaries, and that in several instances only certain sections of the inhabitants were concerned in the election.

Many of the old Harvest customs have disappeared, though most farmers still provide a Mell or Harvest Supper for all their workers after the corn has been brought in. Mechanical reapers and binders have replaced the old hand sickles and have made unnecessary the Lord and Lady of the Harvest, who led the reapers and set the pace for the work. They have also done away with the concerted effort on the part of all concerned to get the last field cut before the neighbouring farmer could cut his, and the nominees shouted by the triumphant labourers when they had succeeded in this attempt, to the effect that "This is to gie notice that Mr. —— has gi'en the seck a turn and sent t'owd hare into Mr. ——'s standing corn." So, too, with the cutting of the last sheaf, once so important a part of the harvest rites; the machine takes it in its stride without the superstitious fear that formerly attended this part of the work. There was in every district a definite reluctance to be the one who cut the last handful, and to evade the undesirable distinction, the men took it in turns to throw their sickles at it. Sometimes a ribbon was tied loosely round the last remaining stalks, and the man who cut it was rewarded with a small sum of money. When the sheaf was eventually cut, it was tied up and decorated, or dressed in woman's clothes, and was brought in triumph to the farmhouse and set in a place of honour at the Mell Supper. It was known as the Maiden, or the Kern Baby, or the Mare; the name given to it was always feminine because it represented the Corn Spirit,

[1] G. L. Gomme, *The Village Community*.

whose last refuge it had been while it was still standing in the field. In Scotland it was called the Maiden if it was cut before Hallowe'en and the Cailleach, or Old Woman, if it was cut after that date. But whatever its name it was sacred; it was dangerous to cut it but, once gathered, it was kept in the farmhouse throughout the year as a guarantee of continued fruitfulness in the fields and the success of next year's harvest.

In pagan times the effigy was made for the entire community rather than for the individual homestead, and in two places at least where the Kern Baby is still made, it is brought to the church instead of the farmhouse. At Little Waltham in Essex and at Whalton in Northumberland the last sheaf is dressed as a female doll, the clothes being made of coloured paper and the head and hands formed by the ears of the corn. It is fixed to a pew in the church during the Harvest Festival. At Overbury in Worcestershire there is no attempt to imitate a human figure, but corn is twisted into the shape of a pyramid and hung in the church porch. It is not renewed every year but only when it is worn out. Here the villagers also make smaller pyramids for themselves and take them back to their homes.

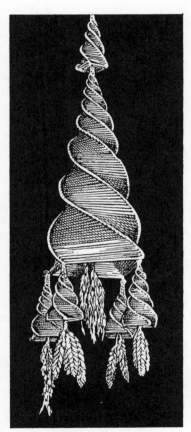

The Kern Baby, Overbury, on Bredon Hill.

The loaves stamped with a sheaf which can often be seen in bakers' shops at harvest time may be a relic of the bread that was brought to church and blessed on Lammas Day, August 1st, the date on which the harvest season was thought to begin. Some authorities derive the word Lammas from "Loaf-Mass" because of this offering, while others consider it comes from a corruption of Lughnassad, the feast of the Celtic sun-god, Lugh Long-hand, which fell on this day. In York formerly it was associated with lambs, and the Minster tenants brought live lambs to the service to be blessed at the High Altar. At one period August 1st was an important agricultural date, for certain lands which had been let to individual holders from Lady Day onwards then became common property once more, and were re-distributed. The term Lammas-land still clings to some fields and pastures as a relic of this custom. Rents were frequently paid then, and in some parts of the country tenants were expected to present their landlords with a pre-scribed quantity of new wheat. Because of this association with payment and the settlement of outstanding dues, the phrase "the latter Lammas" was sometimes applied to the Day of Judgement.

In northern counties, where the harvest comes late, some of the celebrations were held at Hallowe'en and on All Saints' Day. But primarily the rites of these two days were connected with fire and with the dead. Both amongst pagans and Christians the month of November was associated with the cult of the dead; in many districts food was left out for the souls of those who had already died in the family, and the Church honoured the saints in Heaven and the souls in Purgatory on November 1st and 2nd. The first day of the month was also the final end of harvest and the beginning of winter, and bonfires were lit and danced round, as at Midsummer, to strengthen the declining sun. In Lancashire until the end of last century huge fires could be seen on the hills all round the horizon on October 31st, and on the following day burning brands were carried round the fields. Sometimes a farmer would carry a blazing mass of straw to some high ground near his house and throw it up into the air. While it was falling, all present knelt and prayed for their departed relatives and friends. The name "Purgatory Field" still clings to some of the places where this rite was held. In Derbyshire small fires were lit on the commons, and these were said to light the souls going from Purgatory to Heaven. Originally, of course, they were kindled by friction, and the sacred need-fire was carried about the fields in order to fertilise them, just as the ashes of the Midsummer bonfires were spread on the ground for the same purpose.

At Hinton St. George a custom is kept up on the last Thursday

86

in October which may have some association with the fire-rites of this period. The children go round the village asking for candles; it is considered unlucky to refuse their request. The lighted candles are set in lanterns made from mangolds, which often have beautiful and intricate designs upon them, and with these the children parade up and down for about two hours, singing all the time. The anniversary is called Punkie Night, and is believed to be connected in some way with the now obsolete Chiselborough Fair, the exact date of which has been forgotten. Some time ago a new and enthusiastic young policeman tried to stop the parade, but the villagers strongly resented his action and complained to the authorities. The custom was therefore preserved and has been continued ever since.

The bonfires that once blazed at Hallowe'en have now been transferred to November 5th, and are supposed to commemorate the failure of the Gunpowder Plot in 1605. Whether the black-faced children who parade the streets with their "guys" and collect money for fireworks have any very clear notion of the Plot they are celebrating is extremely doubtful, and it is improbable that the men who light bonfires on the hills in the country, or in their back gardens in towns, are deeply interested in seventeenth-century politics. If they fail to give more than a passing thought to Guy Fawkes and his disastrous attempt to blow up the Houses of Parliament, they are probably quite right, for the origin of their bonfires is, as we have seen, much older and more important than that event. At Rippingale in Lincolnshire the bellringers "shoot old Guy" by running down the scale and clanging the bells together. They do this also at Harlington, and here the bellringers have a supper of pork and ale afterwards. A piece of land provides the money for this feast, but no one now knows who gave it. In 1805 a rector of the parish who had quarrelled with his parishioners destroyed many of the old deeds, including that which concerned this land. It is believed that a woman gave it, but nothing more is known about her, and at the annual supper a toast is drunk to "the Unknown Donor."

If the association of November 5th with the Gunpowder Plot is but lightly treated in most places, it is very clearly remembered at Lewes and Bridgewater. In both places the day is marked by processions, religious services, bonfires, fireworks and burning effigies of Guy Fawkes and the Pope. At

87

Lewes the several Bonfire Societies march to the War Memorial, where wreaths are laid and a short service is held. Torchlight processions follow throughout the evening, and towards midnight the great effigies of Pope Paul IV and Guy Fawkes are ceremonially burnt in an open space outside the town. Formerly the burning took place in the streets, and flaming tar-barrels were rolled up and down the roads among the shouting crowds. All attempts to stop the celebrations were entirely useless, and merely resulted in serious riots. In the end it was agreed that the Societies themselves should be responsible for keeping order and preventing damage to property, and this arrangement has worked admirably ever since. The Cliffe Society is the oldest of the six organisations, and possesses an eighteenth-century banner with the words "No Popery" upon it which is still carried in their processions.

One other custom preserves the memory of the deluded Guy Fawkes. Before Parliament opens, either on the previous evening or at ten o'clock in the morning of the actual day, the Yeomen of the Guard search the entire building, beginning with the basement. They carry candle-lanterns with which they peer into every conceivable corner that might conceal a conspirator, regardless of the electric light which has superseded the older form of illumination since the days of the Gunpowder Plot. When they have satisfied themselves that all is well, a message to that effect is sent to the King, and Parliament is then free to assemble without the fear of a second, and perhaps more successful, attempt on the lives of its members.

62 Guy Fawkes' effigies in the streets of London, 150 years ago

From a coloured aquatint by W. H. Pyne

63 An open-air service in the Cotswolds for blessing on the crops

64 Ponies on their way to Barnet Fair

Chapter IX

FAIRS AND WAKES

THE English Fair is one of our most ancient and happy institutions, and fortunately it shows no sign of dying out as yet, in spite of the decline in its commercial value. Many of our existing fairs can show a continuous history of several centuries, and some are considerably older than the Charter which gave them legal status. We know that the Romans had fairs, and it is probable that some were held in England under their rule. Cornelius Walford traces the Helston Fair back to Roman times, as well as some of those held along the line of the Roman Wall in Northumberland. Alfred the Great, to whom so many good things are attributed, is said to have founded fairs and markets in various parts of his kingdom. He may have done so, but it is likely that many already existed in his time without the benefit of royal sanction. As we have seen, the policy of the early Christian Church had turned many ancient pagan festivals into Christian feasts, and had replaced heathen temples by Christian churches. The people continued to meet for worship in the same places, though their prayers were now addressed to a different deity. The patronal festival of the parish church attracted large numbers of people to the church-town, and in their wake followed hawkers and traders who set up booths and stalls, often in the churchyard itself. The people came principally to hear Mass and to perform their religious duties, but once these were over, they gave themselves up, as in the pagan festivals, to games, dancing and other amusements. The day was at once a religious and a secular holiday, and the booths of the merchants added novelty and interest to the occasion and brought considerable profit to their owners.

These early gatherings were not fairs in the true sense, for they had no charter. Often, however, they became such after they had been running for a considerable time. As the trade increased, a charter would be asked for and granted, and the Fair then became established by law. Many of the charters granted by the Norman kings to the monasteries and other

Lords of the Manor confirmed an already well-established fair rather than created a new one. Where no such charter was given, the market frequently continued without it and gained the name of Fair by custom. St. Giles' Fair in Oxford is an instance of this. It sprang from the annual Wakes festival of Walton parish, and has never had a charter, yet it has outlived the regular chartered fairs of the city, and is still one of the largest and best known pleasure fairs in the Midlands (67).

In the Middle Ages, fairs were the great trading events of the year. Some of the most important attracted merchants not only from every part of England but also from France and Flanders and other European countries. They brought enormous revenues to their owners and an unrivalled opportunity of profit and pleasure to those who attended them. While they lasted, the normal Guild regulations forbidding strangers to trade within cities were suspended, and outsiders were allowed to enter and sell their goods without molestation for as long as the fair lasted. An Act passed in 1331 ordered that "every Lord at the Beginning of his Fair shall proclaim how long the fair shall endure" and fixed penalties for any who continued to sell after it was over. The regular courts were superseded by Courts of Pie Powder, at which the regulations were enforced and disputes settled by merchants present at the fair. A Statute of Edward IV lays down:

". . . And to every of the same fairs is of right pertaining courts of pie-powders to minister in the same due justice on his behalf; In which courts it hath been all times accustomed, that every person coming to the same fairs, should have lawful remedy of all manner of contracts, trespasses, covenants, debts, and other deeds made or done within any of the same fairs and within the jurisdiction of the same, and to be tried by merchants being of the same fair."

Most of these courts have now disappeared, but they still exist at St. Bartholomew's Fair in Newbury and at the "Dirty" or October Fair at Market Drayton.

The autumn is the great season for fair, but some are held in the spring or summer. A very interesting celebration is the Whit Monday Charter or "Pole" Fair which takes place at Corby in Northamptonshire every twenty years. It is supposed to commemorate the Charter granted by Queen Elizabeth in

1585 and confirmed by Charles II in 1682. Local legend says that when the Queen was staying with Sir Christopher Hatton at Kirby Hall she was thrown off her horse into a bog. Some men from Corby village rescued her from this unpleasant position, and she showed her gratitude by granting a charter which freed them from various tolls and also from the duty of serving on juries at the Assizes and elsewhere. In memory of this privilege a celebration which by custom has come to be called a Fair is held every twenty years, the last occasion being in 1922 and the next, if the war is over by then, in 1942. The Charter is read by the Rector and the Chairman of the Parish Council, after which all the fun of the fair is in full swing.

The most interesting part of this fair is an ancient custom which has nothing to do with the charter, and the origin of which is obscure. Before the fair opens, every road and lane leading to the village is barred by strong wooden gates surmounted by banners with loyal mottoes. A watch is kept by these barricades, and every person who wishes to enter is stopped and asked to pay toll. If a man is bold enough to refuse he is hoisted on to a pole and carried off to one of the three sets of stocks still standing in the village. They are said to be the only stocks still in use in England. The traveller is then given a second chance, but if he is still obstinate, he can be set in the stocks for a certain period, or until he decides to pay. Appeals to the police are useless, for this is Corby's immemorial privilege on Fair Day. Few, however, let obstinacy carry them so far, and even the meanest traveller finds the threat of this ancient punishment sufficient to loosen his pockets as a rule. A woman has to endure the same penalty except that, as a concession to her sex, she is carried in a chair instead of astride a pole. To motorists from a distance who have never heard of Corby's Fair, this demand with its accompanying threat must come as a considerable surprise; but the publicity given to the 1922 celebration should help intending travellers to remember 1942, and either avoid the village altogether, or else supply themselves with a sufficiency of small change.

An older Whit Monday Fair is that held at St. Ives in Huntingdonshire. It is, in fact, older than the name of the town to which it belongs, and was granted by Henry I in 1100 to the township of Slepe, which belonged at that time to the Abbey of Ramsey. Unlike its namesake in Cornwall, whose patron saint is St. Ia, a lady who crossed from Ireland on a cabbage leaf, St. Ives in Huntingdonshire really is dedicated to the saint of that name. He was buried at Slepe, and a healing spring rose close to his grave; when his bones were removed to Ramsey by Abbot Ednoth, a subordinate monastic house and church were built near the site and dedicated to St. Ive. Later, the growing town took the name of its patron saint, perhaps helped to this decision by the great importance of its fair which was also called after him. Originally this fair was held in Easter Week and lasted for eight days. Its chief trade was in cloth, wool and hides, and Henry III showed his appreciation of its goods by buying large quantities of stuffs for the liveries of his household. In the thirteenth century it was one of the greatest English fairs, with special sections reserved for cloth-shearers and tailors, and another for the canvas merchants. To-day it is held for one day only, on Whit-Monday, and makes up in jollity and noise what it has lost in commercial importance.

Honiton Fair, which dates from 1257, was originally held on Whit-Monday and the two following days. It now takes place on the Tuesday after July 19th. An interesting survival at this fair is the gilt glove on the top of a decorated staff which the Town Crier carries at the opening ceremony. Standing before the assembled crowd, he proclaims:

> Oyez! Oyez! Oyez!
> The Glove is up and the Fair has begun.
> No man shall be arrested
> Until the glove is taken down.
> God Save The King!

The children present repeat each sentence after him, and then scramble for a shower of heated pennies which are thrown to them from the windows of the Angel Hotel.

A wooden hand or glove was once the signal for outside merchants to enter the town, and a guarantee that they might trade there without fear of arrest or punishment for so long as the fair lasted. The Guild laws of the Middle Ages were extremely strict and were designed to keep trade within the hands of Guild members. Outsiders could not buy or sell within the jurisdiction of the Guild except by special permission or during the annual fairs. Even as late as the seventeenth century, the burgesses' oath at Preston included the clause: "You shall know noe foreiner to buy or sell any merchandise,

65 Mop Fair, Stratford-on-Avon

66 Unfurling the flags of the nations at the Shakespeare Memorial ceremony,
Stratford-on-Avon

67 St. Giles' Fair, Oxford, in 1885

with any other foreiner within this town or the franchise thereof except at Faire Time, but you shall warn the Mayor or Bailiff thereof." The glove was the sign that these laws were temporarily suspended. At the Exeter Lammas Fair an enormous stuffed glove was carried in procession through the streets on the top of a long pole decorated with ribbons and flowers. As soon as it was placed on the Guildhall roof, the Fair began. At Southampton a fair held on Trinity Monday was opened by the hoisting of a glove and dissolved by its removal. In Chester a carved and painted wooden hand was displayed on St. Peter's Church during the Summer and Autumn Fairs and was last hung there about the middle of the nineteenth century. The hand, which has a metal ring and hook at the wrist, and bears the words "Hugo Comes Cestria" on one side, and "Guilda de Civit Mercat, MCLIX" on the other, was left in 1867 to the Corporation of Liverpool by a collector who had acquired it. A writer in the *Journal of the Chester Archæological Society* suggests that the origin of this use of a hand or glove was an ancient Saxon custom whereby permission to hold a market or fair had first to be obtained from a local judge and had then to be ratified by the King, who sent one his gloves as a token of his approval.

Hampshire's most famous fair—that of St. Giles in Winchester—has disappeared, but Weyhill Fair, the second in importance, is still held on October 10th. Sheep, horses, cheese and hops were the principal items of trade, and these things are still sold there, though the enormous sums once made by the sheep-dealers are now but a memory. It is said that this fair has been held on the same ground since it first began in the eleventh century. It is possible that some sort of market was held there even before that date, for two very ancient roads cross here—the Tin Road from Cornwall and the Gold Road along which Irish gold was brought to the South Coast and so on to the Continent. One part of the ground is still known as Gold Street. It was at this fair that the well-known wife-selling incident in *The Mayor of Casterbridge* is supposed to have taken place.

At the Star Inn a pair of ram's horns with a metal cup fixed between them is still kept, though they are no longer put to their old use. Until 1890 it was the custom to hold a Horn Supper on the night before the Fair, and to initiate newcomers by a ceremony known as Horning the Colt. The novice was seated in a chair with the horns on his head, the cup between them being filled with ale. All present sang a song which ran

> So swift runs the fox, so cunning runs the fox
> Why shouldn't this heifer grow up to be an ox,
> And get his living among the briars and thorns
> And drink like his daddy with a large pair of horns,
>   Horns, boys, horns, boys, horns,
> And drink like his daddy with a large pair of horns?

The natural history of this ditty seems a little mixed, but doubtless the occasion was none the less enjoyable for that. When the singing was over, the novice drank the ale in the cup, and was then expected to treat the company to half a gallon of beer.

Pack Monday, or St. Michael's Fair is held at Sherborne on the Monday after Old Michaelmas Day, October 10th. In the small hours of the morning, shortly after midnight, a strident din bursts out in the quiet streets, and a mixed band of young people march through the streets blowing bugles, horns, and whistles and banging upon kettles and tea-trays and anything else from which a good hearty noise can be produced. This is "Teddy Rowe's Band," a custom which has persisted for several centuries, and has defied every effort to stamp it out. Its origin is obscure; the local explanation is that Teddy Rowe was the foreman of the masons who were employed on the remodelling of the Abbey Church after the fire in the fifteenth century. When the fine nave fan vault was finished in 1490, he is said to have led the workmen in a noisy and cheerful celebration, which the people of Sherborne have kept up ever since on Fair days. Whether this be the true explanation or not, the custom seems to date at least as far back as the fifteenth century, and up to the outbreak of the present war it was carried on as vigorously and noisily as ever.

Many fairs are named after the principal merchandise sold there. Barnet and Morley have Horse Fairs (65), Exmoor ponies are sold at Bampton Pony Fair, Frome has its Cheese Fair, at the beginning of which cheeses are "christened" in the local stream for luck. Corby in Lincolnshire has a great Sheep Fair, Nottingham and Tavistock have Goose Fairs, and Boston has a Beast Mart for horned cattle on December 11th. Stratford-on-Avon still attracts large numbers of people to its Mop Fair in October (65), and other Statute Hiring Fairs are held in Lincolnshire and elsewhere. At these "Mop" or Hiring

Fairs, servants were formerly hired for the year, usually from Michaelmas to Michaelmas. They stood in a row wearing the signs of their trade, a crook or tuft of wool for a shepherd, a whip for a carter, straw for a cowman, and so on. On being engaged, they were given a "fastenpenny," or earnest-money, and the rest of the day was spent in enjoying themselves at the fair. Here and there a few labourers still offer themselves for employment in this way at the "stattit" fairs, but the custom is fast dying out, and will probably have disappeared entirely in a few years' time.

Ale-tasters were once important manorial officials who had their part to play at fairs as well as at other times. The October Fair at Market Drayton is now usually opened by a shortened version of its traditional ceremony, but the full-dress ceremonial includes constables, searchers, sealers, scavengers and an official ale-taster. The Steward of the Manor, in his scarlet robes, calls upon the ale-taster to read a proclamation in which all thieves, rogues, vagabonds, cutpurses and disorderly persons are warned to depart immediately, and respectable people are promised immunity from arrest except for outlawry, treason and murder. At Dalton-in-Furness, the Steward of the Manor accompanied by two javelin men with halberds, proclaimed the Fair from the steps of the Market Cross. A meeting was then held to elect various juries and to choose two men who would serve as ale-tasters. It was their duty to visit every inn and public-house in the town, and on their report a red ribbon was awarded for the best ale, and a blue ribbon for the second best. The full ceremony was last performed on October 24th, 1925, when the peaceful inhabitants of Furness were forbidden to "bear any habiliment of war, steel coats, bills or battle-axes" or to buy or sell any goods "but by such yards and wands as are, or shall be, delivered unto them by the bailiff of Dalton." Mr. George Umpelby tells me that this fair has almost died out now, and the ribbons have not been awarded since 1925, though unofficial ale-tasting still goes on in the town at the appropriate season.

Three very well-known fairs enjoy a healthy and vigorous life to-day in spite of the fact that they have no known charters and are, therefore, not strictly fairs at all. Mitcham Fair, which is held on August 12th and the two following days, is said to date from the time of Queen Elizabeth, who was always believed to have granted a charter for it. During the opening

95

ceremony a golden key, four and a half feet in length, is held up, and this is referred to in the Official Guide as "The Chartered Fair Key of Mitcham." When, however, inquiries were made before the passing of the Mitcham Urban District Council Act of 1923, the charter could not be traced. The Showmen's Guild were asked to produce it and were unable to do so, and careful search in the Record Office and the British Museum was equally unsuccessful. But whether chartered or otherwise, the fair is extremely popular, as may be seen by the large number of applications for sites and the great crowds which throng to Three Kings Common every August.

Widecombe Fair is known all over the English-speaking world and will continue to be a household word as long as Devonshire voices can sing to the honour of Uncle Tom Cobley and his companions. That small and remote moorland village seems an unlikely place for a fair and, in fact, there is no record that one was ever granted to it. The history of the fair is unknown, or lost, but that does not prevent it from being held every September with all the usual roundabouts and swings and small trade in sheep, cattle and Dartmoor ponies. It is quite possible that Uncle Tom Cobley often visited it in his long lifetime though, as he was a prosperous yeoman, he probably went to it on his own horse, and not on Tom Pearse's grey mare. He lived in the eighteenth century and died at the age of ninety-six, being buried, according to the Registers of Spreyton Church, on March 6th, 1794.

St. Giles' Fair at Oxford is one of those happy and vigorous fairs which are not tucked away in a field but spread themselves over the public streets, cause traffic to be diverted and are really important dates in the town year (67, 68). Oxford once had five chartered fairs, one granted by Henry I to the Priory of St. Frideswide, another given by Edward IV to the Austin Friars and known as May Fair, and three granted by Queen Elizabeth to the City. All have now disappeared, but St. Giles' Fair, which never had a charter, goes steadily on. Sir John Peshall wrote of it in 1773: "At present we have no Fair, a Wake is at S. Giles's called S. Giles's Wake, yearly, the Monday after S. Giles's day." It took place in the Manor of Walton, outside the city walls, and still occupies its traditional site in St. Giles, and Magdalen Street. This Manor belonged in the Middle Ages to Godstow Nunnery and passed to St. John's College after the dissolution of the monasteries. As

Lord of the Manor, this College still takes the fee of 1*s.* for every stake driven into the ground from the standholders in St. Giles, while the City claims the fees from standholders in Magdalen Street. Fruit, cake, sweets and other eatables, china, ironmongery, Woodstock gloves, and a host of other small articles are sold at this fair, but the greater part of the ground is given up to roundabouts, shooting-galleries, games and sideshows, and mechanical contrivances of every kind. In 1939 it was hoped that, in spite of lighting restrictions and an ominous international situation, it might be possible to hold the fair as usual; but the war which broke out on September 3rd came just too soon for it, and its brilliant lights and noisy pleasures, like those of other fairs, had to be postponed to the happier times of future peace.

St. Giles' Fair is not the only survival of old-time Wakes in the country. In Leicestershire the annual village holidays at which an unofficial fair is often seen are known as Wakes, while in the South Midlands they are called Feasts. The word "wake" comes from the custom of "waking" or watching in the church on the eve of the dedication feast. The day itself, with its rush-bearing procession, its Morris dances, games and wrestling and its gingerbread and ribbon "fairings" was the chief annual holiday of the district and was sometimes extended to a festival lasting three or four days. The modern village Wake or Feast is a direct descendant of this custom, and nearly always takes place on or about the patronal festival of the parish. A special service in the church or the ringing of bells serves to remind the revellers of the true origin of their holiday, and in some districts a modified form of rush-bearing is still carried on, either on the day itself or on the following Sunday. In 1536 an Act of Convocation ordered that all wakes should be held on the same day, the first Sunday in October, but in most places habit and old association were too strong for the authorities, and the true date was still honoured, as it is in many places to-day.

In Lancashire and Yorkshire, Wakes are very much alive, though the religious association is now somewhat overlooked. Wakes Week is the great event of the year in many cotton- and wool-manufacturing towns, when the whole town goes on holiday, and the mills and factories and most of the shops are closed. North-country people have always claimed that they work harder and play harder than their southern relatives, and certainly it is only in the north that one can see a whole population celebrating together in this way. Most of the people go away to Blackpool or some other seaside place, where great preparations are made to receive them, and the railway companies encourage this exodus by issuing circular tickets for the week to the various places of interest on their lines. It used to be the custom in many homes, and perhaps still is, to save up all the year for this holiday and, before leaving, to hide enough money in the teapot to pay the rent and carry on till the next pay-day after the family's return. In prosperous times a great deal of money changed hands during these holidays, and even the depression in the cotton and wool trades has not been enough to destroy the northcountryman's healthy capacity for enjoying himself in the time-honoured manner when Wakes Week comes round once more.

Chapter X

MEMORIAL CUSTOMS

WHEN Charles II lay dying in 1685, a vast, unhappy crowd gathered outside the Palace and waited silently in the bitter cold of an exceptional February for news of their King. James Fraser[1] tells us that "for near two hours the report was his Majesty could not recover out of it, which made all persons of all ranks and degrees melt into tears and fall a-crying." This kindly and humorous man, courageous in his misfortunes, pleasant and generous as an individual, wise and tolerant as a monarch, has long been decried by Whig historians, though his true character is coming to be somewhat better appreciated in modern times. To the people of his own day, he was at once friend and protector; his return to England meant not only the restoration of the traditional monarchy and a release from Puritan tyranny, but the return of normal life and all those kindly and happy customs which Cromwell's dictatorship had overshadowed for so long. On that fine morning of May 29th, 1660, when the exiled King rode over London Bridge into his capital, such a wave of joy spread over the whole country as has perhaps never been experienced there before or since. In London itself the streets were hung with tapestry and strewn with flowers; in every village the bells were rung, bonfires were lit and the people ran wild with happiness. They had passed through a bad time and now relief was come in the person of the dark-visaged king on whom so many secret hopes had so long been centred. The Rector of Maids Moreton wrote in his church register: "This day, by the wonderful goodness of God his Sacred Majesty King Charles II was peacefully restored to his martyred father's throne . . . and from this day ancient orders began to be observed. *Laus Deo*," and thereby expressed what most of the new King's subjects felt.

His was a difficult reign, and the rest of it was not so happy as the beginning. But throughout all its troubles he retained

[1] James Fraser, February 5th, 1685, *Egmont*, II, 46.

the affection of the common people and the love and admiration of all who knew him well. His romantic adventures after Worcester, his courage through the years of poverty and eclipse, his generosity to friends and enemies alike after his restoration endeared him to all who were not blinded by political passion, and his memory is still preserved in many parts of his kingdom on Royal Oak Day. Although a comparatively modern king, he has become as firmly enshrined in English folk-custom as King Arthur is in folk-legend, and one cannot help feeling that he would have rejoiced to see the celebration of his birthday and his restoration united, as they often are, with the older rituals of May month, so hated by his Puritan enemies and so dearly loved by his people.

The best known of these memorial ceremonies is that which takes place at the Royal Hospital, Chelsea, on May 29th. Legend has it that it was Nell Gwynne who suggested the building of this hostel for old soldiers who could no longer earn a living for themselves. There is, however, no proof of this, and Charles rarely needed anyone to remind him of his duty to those who had served him well. The Hospital was founded in 1682 and has ever since been a refuge for men who have deserved well of their country in the Army and now need its help in their old age. On Founder's Day, May 29th, the Grinling Gibbons statue of Charles II, which stands in the centre of the main court, is entirely covered with oak boughs, in memory of that fateful day in September 1651 when the young King hid with Colonel Careless in an old oak near Boscobel while the Roundhead soldiers searched the woods all round him. The two cramped and anxious fugitives were forced to remain there all day, not daring to speak or even to shift their uncomfortable positions for fear of being overheard by the soldiers below. The thick veil of leaves saved the King and changed the course of English history, and every pensioner at Chelsea wears a sprig of oak-leaves on Founder's Day as a memorial. In their scarlet coats and cockaded hats they parade for inspection before some special visitor, usually a member of the Royal family or some well-known general, who also wears the oak-leaf. Not all can take part in this or in the march past that follows, for some are cripples who have lost a leg during their war service. But these also are present in their uniforms and wearing all their medals, seated in places specially reserved for them. The cheers that end the little

68   St. Giles' Fair, Oxford, at the present day
(*The flag is* not *at half mast*)

69   The procession of the Garland King and Queen, Castleton, Derbyshire

70   Nelson commemoration in London: the monument wreathed in garlands in Trafalgar Square, on October 21

71   Laying a wreath on the spot where Nelson fell on the quarter-deck of *Victory*, Portsmouth, on Trafalgar Day

ceremony are partly for the visitor, but some of them are for the King who provided this pleasant and peaceful shelter for their declining years in what was then the rural village of Chelsea. The celebration in this case is no mere formality but a real remembrance of one who did not forget those who had served him faithfully or would so serve his successors on the Throne.

Another and older soldiers' hospital, the Leycester Hospital at Warwick, celebrates the Restoration by decorating the rooms and galleries with oak boughs and greenery and by the issue of special rations for the men. In Worcester a civic ceremony is held which includes the hanging of oak branches on the Guildhall gates. In Northampton the citizens have their own reasons for remembering Charles with gratitude for when, in 1675, a large part of the town was destroyed by fire, he gave a thousand tons of timber from Whittlewood Forest to rebuild their houses and also forgave them the payment of chimney tax for seven years. Here, on May 29th, the choristers of All Saints' Church decorate his statue with oak boughs, and the schoolchildren walk in procession with the Mayor and Corporation, carrying bunches of oak-apples and gilded oak-leaves. After the procession has passed through all the principal streets, a service is held in All Saints' Church, and a charity sermon is preached. There were formerly two old charity schools in the town, one for boys and one for girls. The boys' school is closed now, but the girls' school remains, and the scholars still take part in the procession in their blue dresses and white aprons and caps, carrying the oak-apples and gold leaves according to a rule laid down some two hundred years ago.

These civic ceremonies are interesting, but the many folk-customs associated with the Restoration are even more so. The children of Northamptonshire villages still wear sprigs of oak on May 29th and carry bunches of nettles with which they attack anyone bold enough to appear without these signs of loyalty. This is one of the few counties where this custom still survives, but at one time it was found almost everywhere. In Wiltshire and Berkshire the day was known as Shitsack Day; sprigs of oak were worn in the morning and even-ash leaves in the afternoon. All who were not so adorned were thoroughly pinched by those who were. It may be remarked that both the oak and the ash were regarded as lucky trees long before the Restoration, the former being a protector against thunder and lightning and the latter against all manner of witchcraft. The ash is connected with royalty by an old superstition which says that when the crop of ash-keys fails, the King or a member of his family will die. Such a failure is said to have occurred before the execution of Charles I. In Nottinghamshire the day was known as Oak and Nettle Day, because of the nettles which the oak-adorned children carried to chastise those who wore no oak.

Nor was it only the children who wore these loyal sprigs. Their parents and other adults wore them and the houses were decorated with oak boughs. At Whitechurch Canonoricum the men of the village went out at three o'clock in the morning to cut oak branches, one of which was set on the church tower and another on a post in the centre of the village. The bells were then rung and the ringers afterwards went round the village setting boughs over the doors of every house. This custom has not long died out, and though the houses are no longer visited, the church tower was decorated and the bells rung only a few years ago.

Sometimes a long established custom was adapted to serve the general rejoicing. At Shillingstone a maypole on the green is hung with flower-wreaths on or about June 9th, the wreaths being left there until they wither. This is all that now remains of the ancient May-day festivities which formerly included dancing until a late hour round the garlanded maypole, and a sort of unofficial fair, with booths and sideshows. At the time of the Restoration the ceremony was transferred from the more usual date to May 29th, and was put forward a further eleven days, like so many other old customs, with the change of the Calendar in 1752.

The most delightful Restoration celebration still left to us is the procession of the Garland King and his Queen at Castleton (69). The ceremony is obviously much older than the event it is supposed to commemorate and may once have taken place earlier in the month. The garland which the King wears is a large bell of greenery and flowers which completely covers his head and shoulders, and is crowned by a posy known as the "queen." His companion, now also called the Queen, was formerly known as "the woman," and is a man dressed in woman's clothes with his face swathed in a veil. The two ride round the village on flower-decked horses, followed by groups of children who dance before the inns and the principal houses. At the end of the procession, the queen posy is taken off, and the heavy garland is hauled by a rope to the top of the church tower, where it is left. Later in the evening, the local Boy Scouts and the dancers line up to form a guard of honour while the Garland King lays the queen posy at the foot of the War Memorial. The presentation of the posy is the highest honour that the bellringers, who organise this ceremony, can bestow; formerly it was given to some member of an important local family, but now it is more fittingly given to the memory of those who died for their country and their village in the Great War.

One other custom held on May 29th may be mentioned here, though it actually commemorates a battle fought three centuries before Charles II's time. The choir of Durham Cathedral sing an anthem every year on three sides of the cathedral tower, a custom which is said to date from the Battle of Neville's Cross in 1346, when Queen Philippa defeated the advancing Scots under David I. The monks gathered to pray on the tower while the battle was raging, and the custom has been kept up ever since in thanksgiving for the victory. The choir sing on the east, the south, and the west sides; tradition says they do not sing on the north side because a chorister once fell from it and was killed. The battle was fought in October, and there seems no obvious reason why it should be celebrated on May 29th, except, perhaps, the general tendency to associate occasions of rejoicing with the events of that historic day.

Probably no naval leader has ever received so much love and trust from the people of this country as Lord Nelson did in his day. He was their idol, and their chief hope of deliverance from the terror of Napoleon. In Devonshire it was said that he was a reincarnation of Sir Francis Drake. When the fear of the French was at its height, just before he sailed on the voyage from which he never returned, the people of Portsmouth gathered outside the inn where he was staying, and fell upon their knees crying, "Save us, Lord Nelson, save us!" Countess Brownlow tells us in her reminiscences how the news of his death entirely overshadowed the joy of victory for most people, and how the coaches which brought the news had black mourning ribbons on their victory evergreens. To-day he is still the symbol of the true English spirit for most of us, and his memory is honoured every year on October 21st throughout the country. In London wreaths are laid at the foot of his monument in Trafalgar Square (70); an anchor of laurel leaves comes from the descendants of the officers who fought with him at Trafalgar, and bunches of evergreens from the modern ships named after those which took part in the battle. At Portsmouth the *Victory* is decorated with garlands, and Nelson's famous signal is flown by all the ships in the dockyard; a wreath is laid on the *Victory's* deck where he was struck down (71), and a short religious ceremony is held.

Sir Francis Drake is remembered every few years at Burrator, not for the gift of victory over Spain, but for the gift of water. His place in history as a great Admiral and a daring navigator is assured; so is his place in the hearts of the people as a folklore hero, as the legend of Drake's Drum and the many tales of quite incredible achievements will testify. What few people remember is that during a short spell when he was out of favour with the Court, he turned his attention to civic matters and became Mayor of Plymouth. He devoted his boundless energies to improving the town's water supply by bringing water from Dartmoor and laying the foundations of the present Burrator reservoir. Every few years the Mayor and people of Plymouth go to Burrator and there drink to his memory, first in spring water and then in wine, saying as they do so: "May the descendants of him who gave us water never lack wine" (76).

The Shakespeare celebrations at Stratford-on-Avon have grown in the course of years from a local ceremony to an international event. Probably no one would be more surprised than Shakespeare himself if he could see the streets of his native town adorned with the flags and shields of all nations, and pilgrims from Europe, Asia, America and the Dominions walking in procession to lay flowers on his grave. Perhaps he would be a little amused as well as flattered by all this fuss and ceremony, remembering the somewhat different opinion Stratford once held of him in his early days. Now Ambassadors, Ministers, learned men, poets, actors and simple tourists pour into the town on April 23rd to pay him homage. At mid-day the Union Jack on the central flagstaff is unfurled, and a moment later the flags of half the world are broken on the long line of poles stretching down Bridge Street (66). A steady stream of visitors, distinguished and otherwise, visit the birthplace and the church, where masses of lovely wreaths and bunches of flowers are laid upon the grave. The little Warwick-

72   The painted room at 3 Cornmarket, Oxford, formerly the Crown Tavern

73 A new quill pen placed on John Stow's effigy in the Church of St. Andrew Undershaft, London

shire town echoes to the sound of American voices, and the strange syllables of pilgrims from Arabia, India, China, and countries even further away. Shakespeare, like Alfred the Great, in a different sphere, is one of the few men whose greatness no one has ever attempted to deny; even the Baconian theory is based upon recognition of his superlative genius combined with an undemocratic inability to believe that it could have flowered in the mind of one who sprang from simple yeoman stock.

In Oxford on the same day a simpler homage is paid to him. The mayor and representatives of the City and University go from the Town Hall to the Painted Room in Cornmarket and there drink his health in sack and malmsey wine. This little ceremony is quite modern, having been started only in 1938, and springs from the discovery of a room which Shakespeare must often have seen in his time, and where he probably slept on several occasions. No. 3 Cornmarket was once part of some property owned in 1485 by New College. In Shakespeare's time it was a tavern, a house distinct from the ordinary inn, inasmuch as beer was sold at inns and only wine in taverns. No one could keep a tavern in Oxford who was not either a freeman of the City of London or of the City of Oxford. The Crown Tavern, as the house was then called, was occupied by John Davenant, a freeman of the Merchant Taylors' Company in London, and later Mayor of Oxford. He was Shakespeare's friend, and father of Sir William Davenant, the poet, to whom Shakespeare stood godfather on March 3rd, 1606, in St. Martin's Church. Aubrey tells us that John Davenant was a grave and discreet citizen with a beautiful wife "of a very good wit and conversation agreeable," and that "Mr. William Shakespeare was wont to goe into Warwickshire once a yeare, and did commonly in his journey lye at this house in Oxon, where he was exceedingly respected."

In 1927 the house was tenanted by a famous firm of Oxford tailors. Mr. E. W. Attwood decided to turn one of the upper rooms into a workroom. Board of Trade regulations required that the walls should be limewashed and before this could be done thick layers of old wallpapers had to be taken away. Behind the Victorian grate an old fireplace was discovered and above it the letters I. H. S., probably put there in the days when the house was used for New College students and the room itself, perhaps, as a chapel. Further along the wall, paintings were found, and on the north wall oak panelling dating from 1630, and under it a very fine example of mural painting dating from about 1550. Interlaced figures of old gold outlined alternately in black and white form compartments within which are posies of windflowers, Canterbury bells, passion flowers, wild roses, lilies, and bunches of grapes (72). The rich red-orange of the ground work, and the soft greys and pinks, old gold and black and white of the pattern, are as bright and glowing to-day as they were in the days of the Crown Tavern. Along the top of the wall run the words:

> First of thy Rising And last of thi rest
> be thou gods servante for that i hold best
> In the mornynge earlye
> Serve god Devoutlye
> Feare god above allthynge
> and   and the Kynge.

The last two lines are on the east wall, which is also painted as far as the fireplace.

The great interest of this lovely room, apart from the beauty of the paintings, is that Shakespeare almost certainly used it when he visited the house. In a tavern of this kind, the ground floor would be used for the vintner's business, with possibly a kitchen and parlour as well; the first floor would contain the family's own rooms. The Painted Room on the second floor was evidently the best guest-room, and here Shakespeare, the honoured guest and friend of the family, would be housed. He must have known the paintings well, for they were not covered by the oak panelling until 1630, when he had been dead for fourteen years. Through the energy and interest of Mr. Attwood, the room was placed under the care of the Oxford Preservation Trust, and here on April 23rd the representatives of City and University meet to drink Shakespeare's health in wines of his own day, and in surroundings where he must have spent many a happy and peaceful hour with his friends, the Davenants.

The charming custom by which John Stow is remembered perpetuates the great work of his life. He was London's chronicler in the sixteenth century, and his *Summarie* contains a list of all the officials of the city from the Conquest to his own time. His effigy in St. Andrew Undershaft has a pen in its hand and writes for ever in a large ledger. Every year, on or about April 5th, the Lord Mayor of London and the Sheriffs, and the dignitaries of the ward and parish attend a service in the church, and afterwards stand before the monument and offer a prayer of thanksgiving for Stow's work and example. Then the Lord Mayor places a new quill pen in the stone hand, and the august company departs, leaving the old historian still writing in his ledger, and perhaps inscribing their names and offices in some ghostly counterpart of his London chronicle (73).

Dr. Johnson has two commemorations, one in Lichfield where he was born, and the other in Uttoxeter. In Lichfield on September 18th a wreath is laid at the foot of his statue, and the cathedral choir recite his last prayer on the steps of his house and sing some hymns which were sung in his day and which he must have known. On the same day in Uttoxeter the story of his quarrel with his father and his bitter repentance when it was too late is told in a sermon preached in the market place. Michael Johnson had a stall in this market, and his son's refusal to serve there was the cause of a breach between them which was not healed at the time of the old man's death. The Doctor's repentance came too late to mend the quarrel, but he could and did make public penance for his fault, standing bareheaded in the pouring rain for some hours in the place where his father had worked without his help. The school-children of Uttoxeter hear this story every year, as well as they can for the roar of traffic round them, and afterwards one of them lays a wreath on the memorial plaque which marks the spot where Dr. Johnson made his tardy amends.

A curious and complicated deed of trust was drawn up in 1797 by John Knill, for twenty years Collector of Customs at St. Ives in Cornwall. He seems to have been rather a strange individual. In 1779 he and two others embarked upon a search for treasure which a famous Devonshire pirate named Avery was supposed to have hidden in a cave somewhere east of Lizard Point. Knill was a lawyer and he drew up very precise and careful articles of agreement before the treasure hunt began, but this, like the subsequent expeditions and searching round the Lizard, was entirely wasted. A descendant of the pirate was traced and, at a meeting which he was persuaded to attend, he said that Avery had died at Barnstaple in great poverty and that, in his opinion, no such treasure could ever have existed, since the pirate would certainly have drawn upon it before he fell into such distress. The three adventurers were forced to agree with him, and the scheme was regretfully and finally abandoned early in 1782.

Knill then turned his attention to building a mausoleum for himself on Worvas Hill, near St. Ives. This is now locally known as Knill's Steeple. It is a granite pyramid, fifty feet high, which can be seen for miles and serves as a landmark for sailors. He undoubtedly intended to be buried in it, but difficulties about consecration forced him to change his mind, and he now lies in St. Andrew's Church in Holborn. By the deed of trust already mentioned, he provided for its perpetual upkeep, and also arranged for certain sums to be distributed to various people at five-yearly intervals.

The deed provided that every five years, on the feast of St. James the Apostle, ten little girls, not more than ten years old, should dance to the music of a fiddle for fifteen minutes before the mausoleum and afterwards sing the Hundredth Psalm to the tune used in Knill's time in the parish church. £5 was to be equally divided amongst them, and £1 was to be paid to the fiddler. Two widows, aged sixty-four or more, who went with the children, were to receive £2, and £5 was to go to the married couple over sixty years of age, the husband being a tinner, seaman, fisherman or labourer, who had succeeded in rearing the largest number of children without the help of the parish. £5 was to be paid to the best maker of fishing-nets, and a similar sum to the best packer of pilchards for export, and to the two follower boys who had been most diligent and well-behaved during the preceding fishing season.

These sums are still paid every five years on July 25th. The failure of the pilchard fishery has done away with follower boys, and the pilchard packer's money now goes to the best packer or curer of any kind of fish, but the other awards remain substantially unchanged. The day is a festival occasion for St. Ives. The mayor in his scarlet robes of office and the town officials walk in procession to Worvas Hill, preceded by the ten little girls and their fiddler. A large crowd usually gathers to see the children dance in the sunlight on the short turf of the hill-top, and to hear their treble voices wrestling with the Old Hundredth. A civic dinner, for which John Knill provided the funds, along with his other benefactions, rounds off the day for those privileged to attend it. This celebration was last held in 1936 and falls due again in 1941.

On the last Sunday in August an open air service is held in

Eyam in memory of the men and women who died from plague in the terrible summers of 1665 and 1666, and of William Mompesson, their courageous and gallant rector. This Sunday is Wakes Sunday, and it was during Wakes Week that the plague broke out. It spread rapidly through the village until the winter, and then broke out again in the following May. William Mompesson realised that little could be done for Eyam itself, but it was still possible to stop the infection from spreading to other places. He therefore took the heroic step of persuading the villagers voluntarily to imprison themselves within their own boundaries. It says a great deal both for the courage of the people and the trust they had in their rector that those not yet infected willingly gave up all idea of flight and remained where they were until the following October, when the disease died away. The church was closed and services were held in the open air. The parishioners met on Sundays in a hollow called the Delf, and there the rector preached to them from a rock. No one was allowed to enter or leave the village; food was sent by the Earl of Devonshire and left on a stone at a safe distance from which it was fetched later on by the men of the parish. There is no doubt that many of those who died could have saved themselves if they had gone away from the plague-stricken village, but the risk to the surrounding district was too great and they remained. By October two hundred and fifty-nine people had died out of a population of three hundred, amongst them Catharine Mompesson, the rector's wife; of two families, the Hancocks and the Talbots, only one person survived. The sacrifice made by this small village was heroic, but it was not wasted. The plague was kept strictly within the boundaries of Eyam parish, and no single person from beyond those boundaries was infected.

Maidens' Garlands used to be hung in many churches when a young girl of unblemished reputation died. They were usually made of white linen or paper, and decorated with rosettes; some had blue and white streamers and nearly all had a glove or gloves attached to them. They can still be seen in a number of churches (74), but the custom itself seems to have died out, except at Abbotts Ann in Hampshire. Here a garland is still made for any young person of pure life who was born in the parish and died unmarried. In most churches only girls were so honoured, but in Abbotts Ann young lads may also receive a garland. It is made in the form of a mitral crown and is decorated with paper roses. Five white paper gloves hang from it; they represent a challenge to anyone who throws doubt on the good character of the dead person. The garland is carried at the head of the funeral procession by two girls dressed in white, and during the service it is laid upon the coffin. After the burial it is hung at the west end of the church where everyone who comes to the services on the following Sunday must pass under it. Finally it is hung on the wall with a small scutcheon underneath bearing the name, age and funeral date of the dead boy or girl (75).

There are now some forty garlands hanging at Abbotts Ann. There were more, but some have fallen to pieces from old age. The oldest dates from about 1716 when the present church was built, but until recently some cupboards contained others which came from the earlier church. A single garland still hanging at Alne in Yorkshire is dated 1709; another to the memory of Ann Kendall who died in 1715 hangs at South Wingfield. The custom, with its stress on virginity and its crown representing the Virgin's Crown, is undoubtedly of pre-Reformation origin. It lingered on for a long time in Derbyshire, where many churches can still show their garlands, but Abbotts Ann seems to be the only place where it is still kept up.

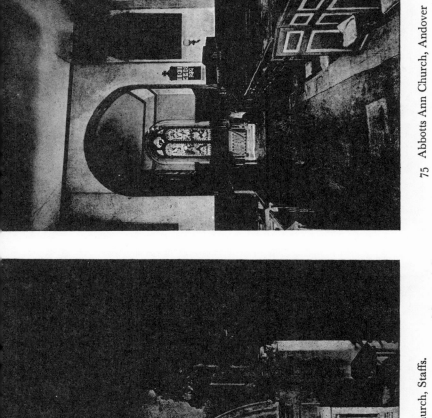

74. Ilam Church, Staffs.

75 Abbotts Ann Church, Andover

Maidens' Garlands

76 Drinking in honour of Sir Francis Drake at Burrator Reservoir, Plymouth

77 The Court and Livery of the Painters' and Stainers' Company in procession
to St. James' Garlickhythe on St. Luke's Day

Chapter XI

CIVIC CUSTOMS

ONE of the most interesting civic ceremonies still existing in England is Preston Guild, which takes place every twenty years and was last held in 1922. It is a survival of the old Guild Merchant meeting, at which the burgesses were called together for the renewal of their freedom and privileges and at which new regulations were sanctioned and old ones amended or repealed. The first recorded meeting was in 1329; this was followed by others at irregular intervals until 1562, when it was decided to hold it once in twenty years, and a by-law to this effect was passed. Round this necessary gathering, called in the first instance for legal business only, gathered a number of festivities not really connected with it, until it became the most important festival of the town, for which an immense amount of preparation was, and is, made and to which people come in their thousands from the surrounding counties whenever it occurs.

Preston's Guild Merchant is believed to have existed by prescriptive right before the town received its first charter, and in the undated *Custumale* of Preston, supposed to have been granted by Henry II, it is said that "no one who is not of that Guild shall make any merchandize in the said town, unless with the will of the burgesses." The mediaeval Guilds exercised a powerful authority over the details of commerce, including the hours of work, the number of apprentices to be admitted to the various trades, the quality and prices of goods sold, the payment of debts and the conditions of labour and marketing. In return they conferred a virtual trading monopoly upon their members, as well as a number of other privileges. In Preston, as elsewhere, no "foreigner" was allowed to trade without permission except, of course, during the annual fairs, and this dislike of strangers extended, even as late as 1616, to their actual residence in the town. A by-law passed in that year ruled that if any householder admitted an outsider, even a friend or a relation, whom the authorities chose to consider "no fytt person" to live in the borough, he had to go within the month; his hosts were required to see that he did go, or else to pay a fine of 6s. 8d. a week for so long as he remained.

In 1565 Queen Elizabeth granted a charter to the town, confirming the rights and privileges bestowed upon it from time to time by her predecessors, and particularly mentioning the Guild Merchant, "with all the liberties and free customs appertaining to such a gild as they have heretofore enjoyed." These rights were re-asserted at the periodical meetings, and the freedom of the burgesses renewed. Cooke, in his *Topography of Lancashire*, says that the Guild was obliged by charter to hold such meetings as otherwise the elective franchise and burgess rights of the townsmen would be lost, but this is a mistake, as no such clause appears in any of the charters. The peculiar privileges of the enrolled burgesses diminished as time went on until by 1835, after the passing of the Municipal Reform Act, all that remained were certain exemptions from toll, the right of turning cattle upon the adjacent moor and marsh, and the exclusive privilege of serving in the corporate offices of the borough. There was some debate as to whether it was worth while to hold the Guild meeting of 1842, the next after the passing of the Act, but fortunately it was decided to do so, and the custom has been kept up in its due season without interruption until the present time.

It takes place in the late summer, and is proclaimed from the Town Hall on three successive Saturdays beforehand. The ceremonies last for several days and are of a very elaborate character. In 1922 the Guild began on Sunday, September 3rd, with the Guild Mayor's visit to the Parish Church and ended on the following Saturday. Formerly the festivities lasted for about a fortnight. In 1802 there were a number of carriage parades, including "more than 200 gentlemen's carriages," and a number of carts bearing working models of cotton machinery and steam engines. The *Monthly Magazine* published a long account of the festivities, the balls, receptions, races on Fulwood Moor, and the two processions, one for men and one for women, which were held on successive days. We read:

"The gentlemen's procession commenced on Monday morning, immediately after breakfast; it was preceded by the Marshal, armed cap-a-pee, on horseback, trumpeters on horseback, etc.; then came twenty-four young, blooming, handsome women belonging to the different cotton mills, dressed in a uniform of peculiar beauty and simplicity. Their dress consisted wholly of the manufacture of the town. The ground petticoats were of fine white calico; the head-dress was a kind of blue feathered wreath, formed very ingeniously of cotton, so as to look like a garland; each girl carried in her hand the branch of an artificial cotton tree, as the symbol of her profession. The gentlemen walked in pairs, preceded by Lord Derby and the Hon. T. Erksine. They amounted to about four hundred, consisting of all the principal noblemen, gentlemen, merchants and manufacturers of this and the neighbouring counties. . . . Upward of a hundred workmen and mechanics followed, two by two. They paraded through all the principal streets of the town, attended by bands of music and flags, with various emblematical devices, etc., and then proceeded to the parish church."

On the following day the ladies had their procession, "all superbly dressed and adorned with a profusion of the richest jewels." The *Monthly Magazine* contributor, perhaps a little carried away by his enthusiasm, tells us that some of their dresses were "said to be worth more than £10,000." The mill-girls led the parade as before, and the streets through which they passed were lined on both sides by the gentlemen who had walked in the procession on the previous day, and now formed a guard of honour for their womenfolk, holding white wands in their hands.

The cotton trade and the gentry were not the only people who took part in these displays, for twenty years afterwards, in 1822, the journeymen tailors refused to walk in the parade because they were placed seventh in the list of thirteen trades represented. They sent in a written protest to the organisers, stressing the antiquity of their craft, and claiming the first place, "which has always been assigned to them from the creation of the world to the present time." Their employers were not so proud, and fifty master-tailors walked in the procession from which all the journeymen were absent.

This six-hundred-year-old celebration is still very much alive, and is carried out with as much magnificence as in the days of the Guild Merchant's power. The display of jewellery and £10,000 dresses has gone, but the processions and other ceremonies are no less interesting and imposing than in former days, and the pride shown in the borough's chief industry is no less marked. To be a freeman of the Guild is now a distinction rather than a commercial necessity; new members are enrolled and old members have their rights confirmed at the Guild Court, after which it is formally adjourned for twenty years.

London's ancient Guilds, or Livery Companies, have preserved many old customs from the time when they were the controlling authorities of the City's trade (77). Several Companies crown their Master and Wardens after they have been elected. The Girdlers use four crowns made of gold and silver thread, with the arms of the Company embroidered upon them. The coronation is announced at the banquet in August, and the crowns are brought in on a velvet cushion, to the sound of music. First the Master is crowned by the Clerk, then the Upper, Middle and Renter Wardens. As the crown is set on the head of each man, his name is called out, and he then drinks to the health of the Company from a large silver loving-cup. The Skinners have a very interesting custom at the coronation of their Master. The crown is first tried on the heads of several people present and taken off again on the ground that it does not fit. When at last it is set on the newly-elected Master's head, it is pronounced to be a perfect fit, and is left in place. This rite is reminiscent of the legendary tests which Celtic candidates for the Kingship had to undergo before they were accepted by the people. The true king had to prove himself by some magical test or ordeal which no other candidate could go through successfully. King Arthur, it will be remembered, was recognised because he alone was able to pull the magic sword out of the stone. At Tara the Irish High King was led to the stone of Fal, which cried out if he were the true claimant and remained silent if he were not. He also had to put on a certain mantle which, like the Skinners' crown, only fitted the rightful ruler. The Fishmongers' Company use crimson caps decorated with silver and, as each new officer is thus "capped," his health is drunk by the retiring Warden.

The annual banquets of the Companies are carried out with all the old traditional rites, including in some cases the ceremonial bringing in of the Boar's Head, with its attendant trumpeters. Every Company has its loving-cup, and while each man drinks from it, the diners on either side of him rise and remain standing until he has finished. In lawless and turbulent ages, a drinker from these heavy cups might well have stood in some danger, for his hands were full and he was not free to draw his sword in case of sudden attack. The men who thus rise at the banquets do so to protect their fellow-member, and the custom is supposed to be in memory of the treacherous murder of Edward the Martyr in 978. He was drinking a stirrup-cup outside Corfe Castle when, as the old chronicle tells us,

> "The knights then pressed upon him, and one seized his right hand, as if to kiss it, whilst another stabbed him on the left. And he exclaimed, 'What do ye, breaking my right arm?', and suddenly fell down dead from his horse."[1]

It is still said at Corfe Castle that the ghost of his terrified horse can sometimes be heard galloping wildly down the steep hill and away into the distance.

On July 12th the Vintners' Company go in procession to St. James's Church, Garlickhythe. The officers carry bouquets of sweet-smelling flowers, and in front of them walk two wine-porters in white smocks and tall hats who sweep the street with besoms. In Edward III's reign, when the Company received its charter, both these customs were very necessary, for every householder threw his rubbish into the streets as a matter of course, and the state of the gutters and the stench that rose from them were alike foul. The Vintners' and Dyers' Companies share what was, in the Middle Ages, a very important privilege, that of owning swans on the Thames. The swan was then a royal bird, and to this day all the swans on the river belong to the King, with the exception of those owned by these two Companies. Each has its Swan Warden, and these officers, with their assistants, meet the Royal Swan Warden at Southwark Bridge on the last Monday in July and go up the river for the annual Swan Upping (78). Every bird has to be caught and examined for its markings to determine ownership; the young ones are then marked, with one nick on the beak if the bird belongs to the Dyers, and with two nicks if it belongs to the Vintners. The King's swans have no marks. The task is by no means an easy one, as the swan is a far from docile bird, and can break a man's arm with a blow from its wing. Swan Upping takes several days, and at the end a Swan Banquet is held, at which roast cygnet is eaten.

[1] Raine, *Historians of the Church of York.*

The Fishmongers' Company are responsible for the arrangements of the annual Thames Watermen's race rowed on August 1st, or as near as possible to that date, for Doggett's Coat and Badge (80). Thomas Doggett was a well-known eighteenth-century actor and a staunch Hanoverian who instituted a race for six watermen, to be held every year on August 1st in honour of George I's accession to the throne. The prize was to be an orange-coloured coat and a badge representing the white horse of Hanover or, as the founder said, "representing Liberty." The first race took place in 1716. Funds for its maintenance were lodged with the Fishmongers' Company, who have since added other sums, so that now every competitor, even the last, who actually reaches the winning post, receives a money prize. The winner gets £10 as well as the coat and badge. The course is from London Bridge to Chelsea, and trial heats are rowed beforehand to reduce the number of competitors to the six originally laid down. The first notice of the race stated that "it will be continued annually on the same day for ever," and if this was perhaps rather a rash assertion, it is at least true that it has been held regularly since its first inception as near to August 1st as the state of the river will permit. It is still as popular as ever, though probably few of the young watermen who take part have any notion that by doing so they are honouring the memory of our first King George, once so admired by the loyal Mr. Doggett.

One of the most important functions of the City's seventy-seven Livery Companies is the election of London's Lord Mayor on Michaelmas Day. This election was originally in the hands of the Aldermen and Sheriffs and of deputations from the Wards. In 1376 the right of choice passed to representatives of the Guilds, and in 1715 it was granted by Act of Parliament to every member of the Livery Companies. The privilege is very jealously guarded and the greatest care is taken to see that no unauthorised person gains access to the Guildhall on the election day. The King Street approach is fenced off and every Company has its beadle in attendance behind the fence to identify the members of the Livery and to challenge any person who cannot produce his credentials. Within the building the Common Crier calls upon all who are not Liverymen to depart before the voting begins, and then calls on the members of the Companies to choose a "fit and able person" to be Lord Mayor for the coming year.

The election is a more dignified and picturesque proceeding than are most similar contests for other positions (81). The Husting platform on which the candidates sit is strewn with flowers and sweet herbs, and the Lord Mayor and Sheriffs, who walk in procession from the Mansion House, are given posies of flowers to hold. Only those Aldermen who have already held the office of Sheriff are eligible. From the names submitted two are chosen by show of hands, the final choice between them resting with the Court of Aldermen. During its deliberations the City sword is laid upon a bed of roses, as a token that the proceedings are secret, and the two candidates are questioned in a whisper. When all have voted, the existing Lord Mayor gives his vote by word of mouth to the Recorder, the Common Sergeant and the Town Clerk and then, with the chosen candidate on his left, he returns to the great Hall, where the final result is announced to the assembled Liverymen by the Recorder.

Before he can take over the duties of his office, the new Lord Mayor has to take the customary oath on November 8th and to receive the diamond sceptre, the Seal of his office, the Purse and the Sword. He has also to go to the House of Lords to receive the King's assent to his election, when the Lord Chancellor drinks his health in a loving-cup containing sack. On the following day the Lord Mayor's Show is held, and on this day the newly-elected Mayors of every borough in the country begin their term of office.

The first printed account of the Lord Mayor's Show appeared in 1585, but these spectacular civic pageants were held long before that. Until 1712 the Lord Mayor rode on horseback in the procession, but in that year a coach was provided for his use. Perhaps the most interesting figures in the old parades were the twin Giants of London, now usually called Gog and Magog, though more properly they should be called Gogmagog and Corinneus. They were so named when Philip and Mary saw them on London Bridge in 1554, and when they were placed at Temple Bar in 1558 to greet Queen Elizabeth on the day before her coronation. With London Stone, they form a link with the legendary origin of the City and with Brutus who, according to tradition, fled from Troy after it had fallen, landed in Cornwall and was there opposed by a band of giants under the leadership of Gogmagog. This giant was overcome by Corinneus, and brought captive to the two small hills between the Fleet River and the Walbrook, where Brutus set up the first London, the mythical city of Troynovant, and built his palace on the site of the present Guildhall. The two wooden figures representing the giant and his conqueror were kept in the Guildhall and perished there in the fire which destroyed much of the building in 1940. They were not those which Mary and Elizabeth saw, but their successors, carved in 1707 by Richard Saunders, the civic carpenter. Since they represented what were long regarded as the guardian giants of the city, it is to be hoped that they will be replaced and set in their old position when the Guildhall is restored.

London's long and sometimes turbulent history is reflected in the curious privileges and rights enjoyed by the Corporation and the Lord Mayor. It is the only city where the Sword and ward maces are carried upright in state processions instead of sloped over the bearer's shoulder, as in other towns. Only those regiments which have descended from the City trained bands—the Buffs, the Royal Fusiliers, the 2nd Battalion of the Gloucesters and the 3rd Battalion of the Grenadier Guards— are allowed to march through the city with bayonets fixed and Colours flying, and no troops may cross the boundary without the Lord Mayor's permission. Even the King has to ask leave to enter the City, a permission granted by the presentation of the City Sword to the King at Temple Bar, in token that the Lord Mayor has surrendered his authority for so long as the King is within his boundaries. Only the King and the Lord Mayor know the password at the Tower, which is changed every night. The Lord Mayor has complete authority over his city, except in two districts, the Temple and Ely Place, which are self-governing. He cannot enter the Temple without the permission of the Benchers, nor can those who come to beat the bounds. Ely Place was once part of the Bishop of Ely's garden and as such was under the authority of the Church. The City had no part in its government and has not now; its gates are locked every evening (82) and it is protected by its own watchman who calls the hours and the weather throughout the night, as town watchmen formerly did everywhere. The police have no right to enter, unless called upon to do so by the Beadle or the inhabitants.

Two interesting old customs are still kept up at Lichfield. In the early fifteenth century the city was required to provide twelve suits of chain armour and two suits of knights' armour

79 The Ripon Hornblower

78 The King's Swan-uppers catching swans near
Windsor

80 The start of the race for Doggett's Coat and Badge at London Bridge

as its contribution to the national defence, and to see that these were always kept in good order and ready for immediate use. A Court of Arraye met annually on Bower Hill to inspect the armour and, though its military responsibilities have long since passed into other hands, it still does so every year in June. The ancient suits are brought out once more and are worn by young lads who parade in them before the city officials and the members of the Court (84). This ceremony is known as Lichfield Bower.

The second custom is the Sheriff's Ride, which takes place on September 8th. It is said to date from the time of Edward VI, and was confirmed by a charter, still in force, which was granted by Charles II in 1664. The Bailiffs and Brethren of Lichfield were directed by this charter to elect a Sheriff on St. James's Day, July 25th, from among those citizens who were not already Brethren. Any reluctance to serve on the part of the elected man was provided for by the power to fine and imprison him if he refused to take office, and to deprive him of all civic privileges. One of his duties was to perambulate the city boundaries once in every year, and this duty he still discharges. Attended by some forty of fifty horsemen, he rides right round the town, halting at the ancient boundary marks, or at those places where such marks formerly stood. This perambulation is quite independent of the ordinary Beating the Bounds which is carried on at Lichfield, as elsewhere, in Rogation Week.

At Ripon the Mayor's Hornblower sounds the city horn every night at nine o'clock in the market place (79), a custom which the inhabitants say dates from the time of Alfred the Great, and which certainly dates from 1400. Before Ripon had a Mayor the principal officer of the town was known as the Wakeman, and the city's motto, painted in large letters across the front of the Town Hall, commemorates him in the words: "Unless Ye Lord Keep Ye Cittie, Ye Wakeman Waketh In Vain." He was required to blow a horn each night at the four corners of the Market Cross as a form of curfew, and also to sound it on the five Horn Days, which fell at Candlemas, Easter, Rogationtide, and on the Feasts of St. Wilfred and St. Stephen. In 1604 Hugh Ripley, the last Wakeman, became the first Mayor, and an official Hornblower was then appointed. The horn now used was given to the city in 1864, but there is an older one which dates from 1690. It is attached to the famous Baldric, a belt on which are a number of heavy silver medallions showing the coats of arms of most of the old Wakemen. It is worn by the Hornblower only on special occasions, when the older horn is sounded instead of the more modern one used every night.

At Bainbridge in Yorkshire another horn is blown at nine o'clock on the green and in the fields in order to guide any traveller who may be lost on the moors. This dread of being benighted in wild places accounts for many of our bell-ringing customs, some of which are supported by charitable bequests. At Twyford in Hampshire the bell-ringers are given an annual feast on October 7th, the funds for which were left by a man who, riding home through the darkness, heard the sound of Twyford bells and changed his direction just in time to save himself from riding over the edge of a deep chalk-pit. He arranged for the bells to be pealed every year on the same date, and for the bell-ringers to have their feast only if this was done. The curfew bell at Kidderminster was continued for a similar reason, a rider coming from Bridgnorth Fair having missed his way and been guided back by its sound. There are many other instances of such bequests made either by people who had themselves been in danger of being lost or who wanted to protect others from such perils. Although the curfew ceased to be compulsory in 1103, it persisted in many places even as late as the middle of last century, and the benefit to travellers may have been one reason for its continuance. In a number of villages to-day a bell is rung from Michaelmas to Lady Day about eight or nine o'clock in the evening, and sometimes the date of the month is rung as well.

One other ancient custom may perhaps be mentioned here, though it is not a civic custom since it concerns not a town but an island. This is the historic Tynwald ceremony in the Isle of Man, the last survival of a meeting of the Thing, or early Scandinavian tribal parliament, left in these islands. Early village or tribal assemblies were nearly always held in the open air, both to allow the people easy access to them, and also from fear of the magic associated with roofed buildings. In Scandinavia the Thing met in an open space, usually near a hill or mound, away from villages or homesteads; those who attended it built themselves temporary booths in which to live while the deliberations lasted. Here laws were promulgated and disputes were settled; bloodshed and violence were forbidden during the sessions on pain of outlawry and death. The Norseman's natural genius for democracy found expression in these open-air parliaments where each man could, and did, give voice to his views without fear or favour, and Norse settlers in other countries kept up the custom wherever they could. In the Isle of Man, once conquered by the Norsemen, the word "Thing" has survived in the name of Tynwald Hill, as it has also survived in the place-name Thingwall which is found in both Lancashire and Cheshire. Tynwald Hill is an artificial mound, traditionally said to be formed of earth brought from the seventeen parishes of the island. It is twelve feet high and has four circular platforms on it. On this hill the titles of the bills passed during the previous year are read out on July 5th, Old Midsummer Day, first in English and then in Manx, and only when this has been done is any law valid in the island.

An early fifteenth-century document, quoted by William Radcliffe in his *Guide to the Isle of Man*, says:

"This is the Constitution of old time, how yee shall be governed on Tynwald Day. First you shall come hither in your array, as a king ought to do, by the perogratives and royalties of the land of Manne. And upon the Hill of Tynwald sitt in a chaire covered with a royall cloath and cushons, and your visage unto the east, and your sword before you holden with the point upwards. Your Barrons in the third degree sitting beside you, and your beneficed men and your Deemsters before you sitting, and your clarke, your knights, esquires and yeomen about you in the third degree, and your worthiest men in your land to be called in before your Deemsters if you will ask anything of them, and to hear the government of your land and your will; and the commons to stand without the circle of the Hill with their clarkes in their surplices. . . .

Then the chief Coroner, that is the Coroner of Glenfaba, shall make affence upon pain of life and lyme, that noe man shall make any disturbance or stirr in the time of Tynwald, or any murmur or rising in the King's presence, upon pain of hanging or drawing, and then to proceed in your matters that touch the government in your land of Manne."

To-day the ceremony is very much as it was hundreds of years ago, with a few modifications. After a service in St.

John's Church, the Lieutenant-Governor, representing the King, heads a procession to the Hill, preceded by his Sword-bearer with the thirteenth-century Sword of State. He passes up the rush-strewn steps of the Hill and seats himself in a red velvet chair on the topmost platform, looking eastwards as the old tradition directs. Beside him sits the Bishop, the last of the Island Barons; the Deemsters and members of the Council stand round them. On the platform below the twenty-four members of the House of Keys are grouped, and on the third platform stand the clergy, the members of the Bar and the High Bailiffs. The fourth and lowest platform holds the minor officials, and round the Hill stand the people of the island. Thus every section of the population is represented.

The Coroner of Glenfaba then rises to "fence" the Court. As at the old meetings of the Thing no man might break the peace on pain of death, so on Tynwald Day all manner of brawls or quarrels are forbidden and "the King of Man and his officers" are protected by the threefold announcement that the Court is fenced. Formerly every bill passed during the year was read in full, but now only an abstract of each is given, in English by the First Deemster and in Manx by the Senior Coroner. The new Coroners, or sheriffs, are then sworn in and receive their wands of office, and finally the people signify their assent to the bills passed in their name by giving three cheers for the King. The procession then re-forms and returns to the Church, where the bills are signed by the Lieutenant-Governor. And so ends this ancient democratic meeting which, though modified in many ways since it was first held on Tynwald Hill, would still, except for the language, be recognised as something familiar and understandable by the tenth-century Viking, if such a man could return to witness it in the present year of grace.

81 Election of the Lord Mayor of London by the Court of Aldermen
in the Guildhall

82　The watchman locks up for the night at Ely Place, Holborn

Chapter XII

THE LAND AND ITS TENANTS

THE ownership and tenancy of land has always been a matter of supreme importance at once to the individuals concerned and to the community at large. From the earliest beginnings of civilised life the distribution of land has been hedged about with protective laws and binding customs, which varied from century to century according to the economic needs of the time, but which always had one object, that of protecting the land itself and the rights of those who lived and worked upon it. This is understandable since, in the final resort, the source of all our wealth is the earth and its products, what grows upon it and what lies hidden within it. The Americans rightly call land "real estate," the one possession that endures and does not perish with the lapse of time, nor cease to yield its fruits so long as care and labour are expended upon it. On its continued fruitfulness depends every enterprise and every advance, and the man who owns it and he who works upon it together support the whole framework of society and civilisation.

In the course of centuries many changing laws and regulations concerning ownership and tenancy, the rights of pasturage and turbary, commons and forest land, have been passed and repealed; changing economic conditions have swept away old established customs and new ideas have helped to transfer power from one section of the community to another. But these changes have usually been gradual, as most changes are in England, and many old customs still survive to remind us of the habits of our ancestors. Manorial courts exist in a number of districts and carry out at least a part of their old duties; the lords of many manors hold their lands by the discharge of some traditional duty, or the payment of such curious rents as a red rose or a pound of peppercorns, and the rights of tenants to certain privileges are still maintained by ancient customs punctually carried out on a given day, according to the practice of centuries.

One of the most interesting of these customs is that which takes place on May 29th at Wishford in Wiltshire. The villagers have the right to gather dry wood in the Forest of Grovely and, once in the year, to cut the largest branch of green wood they can carry. On Oak Apple Day the men rise before dawn and go to the woods to cut oak boughs. They march up the village street with drums and bugles and a banner bearing the words "Grovely, Grovely and all Grovely!" (86). They stop outside every house and shout the words, and those within look out of their windows and greet them. The company then go on to the forest, and when they have gathered their boughs, they return and set them up before the doors of the houses. At noon a procession forms under a tree at the south end of the village. A band goes first, and behind it come four women with faggots on their heads (87); then follow children in fancy dress and men carrying oak boughs. They march all round the village and up to the rectory, shouting "Grovely, Grovely and all Grovely!" as they go. After the procession there is a dinner in a marquee near the Oak Apple Inn, and the rest of the day is given up to sports and amusements of every kind.

This custom is necessary to preserve the ancient right of gathering wood, and a local society fines anyone who neglects to cut a branch on the appointed day, for other parishes have been known to lose their ancient rights through neglect of the customary ceremonies. The boughs have to be gathered "by strength of people," and may not be brought in by mechanical means. It is permissible to use hand-carts and, after some debate, bicycles have been allowed, since they are propelled by human strength, but horse-carts and, of course, motor-cars are strictly forbidden.

An interesting document usually known as the Book of Rights was drawn up in 1603 and signed by a number of local men, one of whom bore the curious name of Stephen Catkat. It set forth the rights "which the Lords, Freeholders, Tenants and Inhabitants of Great Wishford and Barford St. Martin have and ought to have in Grovely," and describes the customs by which they are maintained. Some of these privileges have been lost or commuted for money payments, but the right to "gather and bring away all kinds of snapping wood and boughs and sticks at any time" still remains. The document mentions one most interesting part of the annual ceremony which is now obsolete, the dance in front of Salisbury Cathedral. The people used to go, in early times on Whit Tuesday and after the Restoration on May 29th, to the Cathedral, dressed in white and carrying oak boughs in their hands, and there dance before the church and claim their rights in the traditional words. This dance was regularly given until the beginning of the nineteenth century, when it was suppressed because it gave rise to unseemly revelry in the Close. Grace Read, who died in 1871 at the age of eighty-eight, was the last person to remember it from the days of her youth when she took part in the dance. The Close used to be filled with booths and side-shows and a sort of unofficial fair was held which ended by giving offence to the authorities. But for several years after the actual dance had been transferred to the ground outside Wishford Rectory, two women used to go to the Cathedral as a deputation from the bough-gatherers and reverently lay oak branches on the High Altar.

One object carried in the modern procession is of interest because it commemorates a persistent local tradition. This is a sieve containing seven dolls which represent the seven children born at a birth to Edith Bonham in the fifteenth century. The story is that she had twins, an event which so upset her husband, Thomas Bonham, that he went on a pilgrimage for seven years, during which time he neither communicated with her nor cut his hair or nails. He was warned by a witch that she had given him up for dead and was about to marry again, and he therefore returned home in great haste to prevent the marriage. It is perhaps not surprising that she did not recognise him at first, but when he produced the half of a ring he had broken with her before he left, she acknowledged him as her long-lost husband. In the following year she gave birth to seven children who were taken to church to be baptised in a sieve. This sieve, or "chardger" as Aubrey calls it, was hung on two nails in the church; in 1828 three old people of the parish told James Goulden, the schoolmaster, that they remembered it hanging there in their youth. It has gone now, and so have all but three of the nine brass effigies of the Bonham children which once formed part of their parents' monument. The marks of the other six are still plainly to be seen, though the brasses themselves have disappeared. A kneeling figure apparently whispering in the ear of Thomas Bonham's effigy is popularly supposed to be that of the witch who warned him of his wife's intended re-marriage.

Probably the nine brasses simply represented the number of children in the Bonham family, but the story of the seven born at one time is firmly believed in Wishford. The legend occurs in other places also, the number of children generally being the mystic seven, and always coinciding with the number of years the husband was absent. It is told at Upton Scudamore, also in Wiltshire, and at Chulmleigh in Devonshire. In the latter place the husband was a poor man, unlike Thomas Bonham, who was Lord of the Manor. He was so horrified at the prospect of having to feed and rear so many at once that he put all the babies into a bag and set out to drown them in the nearest pond. On the way he was stopped by the Countess of Devon who insisted on seeing what was in the bag, in spite of his assurance that it contained only puppies. She took the poor, unwanted children to the church and founded seven prebends in the parish for their support; these prebends are now consolidated with the rectory. The multiple births are probably mythical, but the stories themselves throw a strange light on domestic life at a time when men did suddenly depart on lengthy pilgrimages, impelled by religious devotion, disgust with this world, or repentance for some crime, often staying away for years at a time, and leaving their unfortunate wives without news of any kind and with no knowledge whether their husbands were alive or dead.

Wroth Silver is paid on St. Martin's Day, November 11th, to preserve the ancient right of people in a number of parishes in Knightlow Hundred to drive cattle across the Duke of Buccleuch's land. In early times when roads were very bad and all travelling was dangerous, this privilege was highly valuable, and the payments are believed to have been made at the same time and place for many centuries. Originally they were made to the King, but Charles I granted the right to receive them to the ancestor of the present Duke of Buccleuch, and they have been regularly paid to the family since that time. The word "wroth" is generally considered to be of Anglo-Saxon origin, from roots meaning either a road or way, according to some authorities, or cattle money, according to others. The custom itself may possibly date from Anglo-Saxon times also.

The dues now paid vary from 1*d.* to 2*s.* 3½*d.*, trifling sums to-day but worth very much more when the amounts were first fixed. Those concerned are summoned to meet the Duke's steward at seven in the morning, before sunrise according to old tradition, on Knightlow Hill. Each man throws his money into a hollow in the stone which is all that remains of Knightlow Cross, saying "Wroth Silver," as he does so. Afterwards all are given breakfast at the Dun Cow Inn at Dunchurch, and the Duke's health is drunk in rum and milk. As the total sum collected only amounts to 9s. 4d., the Duke is considerably out of pocket at the end of the transaction, but payment is rigidly enforced, and the penalty for default is 20s. for every penny due and a white bull with red ears and a red nose. Such an animal would be almost impossible to obtain to-day, unless perhaps from the Chillingham herd; the prescribed colours are interesting because they are so strongly reminiscent of those legends of fairy white and dun cows which were once supposed to wander through Britain, giving illimitable supplies of milk, and of which the Dun Cow of Warwick is a famous example.

Ratby Feast is held every year on Whit Monday to celebrate the gift of certain lands by John of Gaunt. The story concerning this feast is a charming one, and shows the Duke of Lancaster in a very amiable light. In the fourteenth century the holders of some lot meadows adjoining the high road used to mow them on a day known as Meadow Morning and afterwards dance in the fields. John of Gaunt saw them as he was riding past on his way to Leicester and asked them what they were doing. They told him they had been mowing Ramsdale meadow and were now dancing, according to their custom. Tradition says that the Duke got off his horse and danced with them and, when he was leaving, promised that, if they would meet him in Leicester, he would give them a ewe for their ram and a wether whose fleece would provide them with an annual feast. They therefore went to Leicester and received the grant of three fields, to be called The Ewes, The Boots and The Wether, from the last of which the grass was to be sold on Whit Monday to pay for the meal.

With the fields they received minute instructions about the feast itself. They were to appoint two caterers whose duty it would be to arrange for a breakfast and a dinner at any inn they chose in Leicester. The innkeeper was to give them a calf's head for their breakfast, the bones of which, when picked clean, were to be served again at dinner, a large pie for the caterers' families, and a silk lace tagged with silver for every man present. After breakfast the grass was to be sold at Enderby, and then the whole party was to return to Leicester, wearing the silk laces in their hats, with a piece of grass tied round each one. The laces were to be thrown to the people of the town at the High Cross. There was to be a sermon in St. Mary's Church, which was to be specially decorated with flowers for the occasion, and the deed of gift was to be read during the service. Afterwards the men were to go to the inn for dinner, and the rest of the day was to be spent in feasting and general enjoyment.

Much of this programme is still followed. Only one caterer is now elected, and the breakfast in Leicester has been changed to a lunch at Enderby. It consists chiefly of various kinds of cheese, salads, cakes, and ale. After lunch the grass from The Wether is sold, and then the caterer and seventeen other men ride into Leicester to dine at the chosen inn and drink the health of John of Gaunt in old brandy. At one time they used to ride through the River Soar on their way in because of the old saying that this river, when in flood, "washes the wether's breech," but this is no longer done. The meal, which always includes the calf's head specially mentioned by the Duke, and the provisions for a convivial evening afterwards, are paid for from the grass-sale money, and so is a lunch given to ten inmates of Trinity Hospital which was founded by Henry of Lancaster, John of Gaunt's son.

Many lands are still held either by the performance on special occasions of some service, or by the presentation of a particular object on a particular date. These services or dues may lapse for years because they are not demanded, but unless they are legally abolished they continue to exist and may be revived at any time. When in December 1937 the King visited Launceston Castle, the old ceremonies were carried out in full, and the landholders assembled to deliver a variety of curious things to their Lord and to receive white wands in exchange in token that the prescribed payment in kind had been made. One man brought a pair of greyhounds, another a grey cloak (85), a third a salmon spear; gloves, spurs, faggots, pepper and cummin were among the dues paid for lands which had been so held by successive owners for centuries.

Savernake Forest was granted to the Ailesbury family by the service of blowing a horn when the King comes to visit the estate. This service of cornage was very common and exists in several places. The Downes of Taxal were required to blow a horn on Midsummer Day, "standing on the heights of Windgather," and to hold the King's stirrup whenever he came to hunt in Macclesfield Forest. The Lord of the Manor of Hoton also had to hold his stirrup when he mounted his horse at Carlisle Castle. Wyfold Court was held by the presentation of a red rose whenever the King happened to pass that way on May-day. These, and many other similar services and presentations, are rarely demanded, but there is no doubt that they would be rendered, and probably could be enforced, should the occasion for them ever arise. The Duke of Wellington pays annually for Strathsfieldsaye by the presentation of a tricolour flag on Waterloo Day, June 18th. This flag is hung over the bust of his great ancestor in the Guard Room of Windsor Castle, and near it hangs another, bearing the Fleur de Lys in gold on a white ground, which is given by the Duke of Marlborough on August 2nd, the anniversary of the Battle of Blenheim, as quit-rent for Blenheim Palace.

The City of London annually pays quit-rent to the King's Remembrancer in October for two holdings, one at Eardington in Shropshire, knows as The Moors, and another called The Forge in St. Clement Danes parish. These quit-rents have to be paid between Michaelmas and Martinmas; both are known to have been rendered at least as far back as the thirteenth century, and they may be even older. Originally the tenant of The Moors had to produce two knives, one sharp enough to cut a hazel stick in two at a blow, and the other so blunt that it would make little or no mark upon it. At some forgotten period the knives were superseded by a billhook and hatchet, and these implements are presented to-day by the City Solicitor who chops two small faggots with them. When he has finished, the King's Remembrancer says "Good Service," and the Solicitor hands over the tools.

The Forge has then to be paid for by six enormous horseshoes and sixty-one nails, which must be counted out, and are received with the words "Good Number." The Forge itself has long since disappeared and even its site is a matter of some doubt. It is believed to have stood either where Australia House now stands or on the roadway in front of that building. Walter le Brun, a farrier, paid six horseshoes and sixty-one nails for it in 1235, and though it has long since ceased to exist the same rent is punctually provided for it now by the

Corporation of the City of London. The horseshoes and nails are kept during the year in the office of the King's Remembrancer and are returned to the City authorities every October for the rent ceremony. The hatchet and billhook, however, are not thus preserved, and new ones have to be produced on each occasion.

Candle Auctions are still held in several places, usually for land connected with the church or with some charity. At Aldermaston in Berkshire the Church Acre is let every three years in this way. A tallow candle is provided and a pin is inserted in it an inch below the flame. The vicar conducts the auction, and the man who makes the last bid before the pin falls out becomes the holder of the meadow for the next three years. The rent is paid to the vicar and churchwardens for the expenses of the church. At Tatworth, near Chard, the bidding takes place every year, and is followed by a supper of bread and cheese and onions. At Chedzoy the candle auction is held every twenty-one years, the next falling due in 1946. In both these places no pin is used, but the candle is allowed to burn out, and the last bid made before darkness falls on the room is the successful one. In the same county, at Congresbury, two pieces of land called East and West Dolemoors are annually disposed of by the distribution of marked apples from a bag. Each mark denotes a certain acre, and the land so indicated falls to the man who receives the apple which bears that sign. Afterward four remaining acres are let by candle auction.

At Bourne two boys run races while the bidding takes place for a certain field which Richard Clay left in the eighteenth century to provide loaves of bread for the poor of the Eastgate district. As soon as a bid is made, the boys start running and they have to keep it up as long as the bidding lasts. If they can get back to their starting-point before another offer is received, the last one stands and its maker acquires the land for a year. They are paid a shilling each for their exertions, which are often quite strenuous if the competition is at all lively. This auction is held at Easter and, like that at Tatworth, is followed by a supper.

At Wishford the clerk of the parish goes to the church porch on Rogation Monday at five minutes to seven in the evening and auctions the grass of two plots of land, using the church key as a hammer. He walks up and down between the porch and the gate, and bidding goes on for as long as the sun remains above the horizon. As soon as it sets he strikes the gate with the

83 Archery at the annual meeting of the Woodmen of Arden, Meriden, Warwickshire

84 The Lichfield Bower ceremony: youths parading in the ancient suits of armour

85 Mrs. Rolt presenting to King George VI, at Launceston, a grey cloak provided by Viscount Clifden, from the Manor of Cabilla

key, and the maker of the last bid received before he does so
becomes the owner of the grass until the following November.
This custom is known as the sale of the Midsummer Tithes.

The old manorial courts still function in many districts to
regulate such matters as rents and tenures, the state of roads
and houses, and other questions affecting the lives of those
who live in the districts covered by their jurisdiction. Many
local matters are thus amicably settled which might otherwise
lead to disputes between landlord and tenant, and it would be
a great loss to more than antiquarians if these ancient courts
were finally abolished. Courts Leet and Courts Baron are
often held together, though formerly their functions were
separate, the former being a court of record, with power to
inquire into cases of felony, and the latter dealing strictly with
manorial rights. Mr. James Bushell, writing from Ashton-
under-Lyne, says the Court Leet is regularly held there, with
its Mayor of the Manor, High Constables, Pounder, Ale-taster
and jurymen, "to hear presentments from the farmers to the
landowner, viz., repairs of rural roads, rights of way, etc., thus
saving litigation, and being acknowledged and acted upon."
On rent-day there is a farmers' dinner at which the Mayor of
the Manor, wearing his chain of office, is present, and during
which the Mace is exposed. At Cricklade the Court Leet, or
Reeve Leet, is held to regulate the still existing right of every
householder in the borough to turn out nine head of cattle to
graze on North Meadow between August and February, and
thirty sheep between September and February.

In the New Forest the rights and privileges of the inhabitants
are controlled by the Court of Swainmote which meets at
Lyndhurst. It is composed of seven Verderers and is usually
known as the Verderers' Court. It deals with all matters
which are covered by the forest laws, such as game offences,
the collection or sale of firewood, beech-mast eaten by the
commoners' pigs, the rights of pasturage and turbary, and so
on. Turbary is an ancient privilege belonging to the forest-
dwellers, whereby each householder may take a given number
of turves for his fire, the number allowed to him being governed
by the size of his fireplace. These have to be open hearths, and
the old, wide fireplaces are carefully preserved even in houses
that have been otherwise modernised in order to maintain the
right. There is also a Verderers' Court in the Forest of Dean,
which meets regularly at the Speech House.

The Savoy Liberty in London has its Court Leet to deal
with questions affecting the safety and order of the buildings
in the area and the rights of their inhabitants. Disorderly
conduct within the boundaries, neglect of houses, and kindred
offences can be punished by fines, the amount of which is fixed
by the jurymen. The lords of many manors where Courts
Baron are held still have the right to fine those who do not
attend the Court after they have been duly summoned. The
amount payable is usually quite small, though not in every
case; probably the least alarming of these old fines is that at
Hungerford, where non-attendance at the Sandon Fee Court,
held at Hocktide, involves a penalty of one penny, which is
often given directly to the Town Crier as he goes on his round
to summon the commoners. It must be remembered, however,
that in most cases these sums have not been increased for
centuries, and that what is now worth only a trifle was a much
more valuable sum when the fines were first fixed.

A very peculiar custom existed at Rochford in Essex until
the end of last century. A meeting known as the Great Lawless
Court was held at cockcrow on the Wednesday after Michaelmas in a field called the King's Hill. A post stood in this field,
and to it came the steward and tenants, accompanied by a
torch-bearer whose torch provided the only illumination, as
those present were not allowed to carry lanterns. The tenants'
names were called and answered in a whisper, and the quit-
rents and other dues were paid over in complete silence. A
coal was used instead of pen and ink for whatever writing had
to be done. Originally this curious ceremony took place at
Rayleigh, but it was transferred to Rochford by the command
of the Earl of Warwick. A field was named King's Hill after
the first meeting place at Rayleigh, and a post was set up in
imitation of the one used there. A similar meeting, known as
the Little Lawless Court, used to take place at Hocktide, but
this seems to have lapsed at some period, while the Great
Lawless Court continued to be held until quite recently.

The origin of this curious rite is very obscure. Legend says
it arose because the Lord ot he Manor overheard his tenants
conspiring against him, and ordered them to assemble every
year in darkness and silence on the same night and in the same
place as a punishment. This does not, however, explain why
there should have been two such meetings on different dates,
and the fact that the Michaelmas meeting was preceded by a

supper hardly bears out the idea of punishment. Moreover, this is not the only Lawless Court known to have existed. Another was held at Epping under a certain maple tree which grew between the church and Eppingbury. The use of a tree as a meeting-place here suggests that the post round which the tenants met, first at Rayleigh and later at Rochford, may have been a symbol of some earlier tree under which the court was originally held, and that both customs may have sprung from primitive folk-gatherings under a guardian tree. C. R. Barrett in his *Essex* points out that, although of late years the Great Lawless Court degenerated into a sort of revel, with much cock-crowing and lantern-carrying, this was entirely against the original intention of the court, which was undoubtedly held in all seriousness, and non-attendance at which was punished by heavy fines. He adds that the name Lawless probably arose from the unlawful and weird hour at which it took place, or possibly from the words at the beginning of the Court Roll:

Curia de Domino Rege
Dicta sine Lege
Tenta est ibidem
Per ejusdem consuetudinem, etc.

but this in itself does not explain the whispered roll call, the silent payments, or the writing with a piece of coal. The lapse of this curious survival at the end of last century was probably hastened by the fact that it was no longer taken seriously and had become a mere burlesque rendering of what must once have been a rather awe-inspiring ceremony in the cold and shadowy half-light of an early autumn morning.

A custom known as Kellums once prevailed at Kidderminster during the election of the new Bailiff. An hour between the end of the retiring Bailiff's term of office and the beginning of his successor's term was called the "Lawless Hour," and during it the inhabitants thronged the streets and threw cabbage-stalks at each other. The Bailiff-elect went to pay a ceremonial visit to his predecessor, accompanied not only by the other members of the Corporation and a drum and fife band, but also by an unruly mob of citizens who pelted all in the procession with apples. The *Gentleman's Magazine* for 1790 says that "the most respectable families in the town" took part in this peculiar rite, which was not abolished until the end of the eighteenth century.

The Woodmen of Arden meet every year at Meriden for

their Wardmote, at which an archery competition is held (83). Some such meeting has probably been held there for centuries, for this village stands in the middle of the once vast Forest of Arden, and is the most likely place for meetings held to discuss the rights and duties of the foresters. In 1785 the various groups of woodmen combined into one company, known as the Woodmen of Arden, and to-day the members attend their annual meeting in August in eighteenth-century dress, green coats with gilt buttons, and white trousers. They use a six-foot yew bow, of the type seen at Crecy and Agincourt, and their arrows are stamped according to their weight in silver, as they were in the Middle Ages. Archery was then of supreme importance in battle, and shooting practice was enforced in most towns. Land was set aside for this purpose, and the word "butts" in many place-names preserves the memory of these old shooting-grounds. Newington Butts, in South London, now a mass of shops and houses, was the open space where the City apprentices went for their compulsory practices. In the records of the Manor of Edgware we read that a Court held in 1555 noted that the butts were in a ruinous condition and ought to be repaired by the inhabitants, "which was ordered to be done before the ensuing Whitsontide." By then, however, archery was beginning to decline in importance with the advent of new weapons; in earlier times the butts would never have been allowed to fall into such disrepair.

As we have already seen, the ancient office of Town Crier is by no means extinct, in spite of newspapers, billposters and loud-speakers. Many towns and cities still have their official Criers who, before the majority of people could read, were very important and useful officers of the borough or manor courts. A Town Criers' competition is held in June of each year at Pewsey in Wiltshire. The competitors attend in their uniforms and with their handbells, and prizes are offered for the clearest and most carrying voice and the smartest and best-kept dress. The uniforms vary considerably; some are very ornate, and nearly all are distinctive and dignified, reminding us of the more unhurried age in which they were designed. For most of us, perhaps, the most interesting point about this annual competition is the large number of competitors who attend from all parts of the country, a clear proof of the continued and active existence of this ancient office in many different districts.

86 Grovely procession, Wishford, Wiltshire on May 29th

87 Grovely procession, Wishford, Wiltshire (May 29th): Women with faggots on their heads

88 The Good Friday dole at St. Bartholomew's, Smithfield: widows picking up sixpences from a tombstone

Chapter XIII

GIFTS AND BEQUESTS

SOME of our existing charities are of considerable age, and two at least have come down to us from mediaeval times. The relief of distress has always been considered the first duty of a Christian, as indeed it is for the devout of most faiths. In the Middle Ages, when, in spite of much brutality and harshness, religion really was the central fact of most people's lives, money was freely given and lands bequeathed for the purpose. The Church was then the great dispenser of charity, and rich people left their wealth to found monasteries and chantries which, in their turn, assisted the poor both materially and spiritually. Frequently also direct gifts were made to the poor of a given district, and these often took the form of lands to provide for annual distributions of food or clothing, or shelters for the homeless. Pilgrims on their way to the various shrines of England and the Continent, and other travellers, were helped in some places by daily doles, such as that which still survives at St. Cross, near Winchester. These pious gifts served the double purpose of aiding the distressed and obtaining their prayers for the soul of the donor. The dissolution of the monasteries in the reign of Henry VIII, and of the chantries in that of Edward VI, swept away much money originally intended for charitable purposes, but some of the older personal bequests survived, and a few, in their original or modified form, are still in force to-day.

The Tichborne Dole is given regularly every year on March 25th in accordance with the dying wish of Lady Mabella, or Isabella, Tichborne, as it has been since her death in the reign of Henry I. She was the heiress of Limerston in the Isle of Wight, and wife of Sir Roger Tichborne. Legend says she was a very charitable woman who was greatly loved by the poor of her husband's estates. His character was apparently less kindly, and when she was dying she was greatly troubled by the thought of what would happen to her people when she was gone. She therefore begged him to set aside a piece of land to provide an annual dole of bread on Lady Day. His reply was to take a burning faggot from the hearth and tell her she might have as much land for the purpose as she could walk round while the flame still burned.

In her dying condition this practically amounted to a refusal but, in spite of her weakness, she ordered her maids to carry her outside. Then, finding she could not walk, she started to crawl over the ground and managed to cover twenty-three acres before the flame went out. This land is still known as The Crawls. Before she died she told her husband that if he or any of his descendants stopped the dole, the family would die out and the name of Tichborne would be changed. As a sign of the coming doom, a generation of seven sons would be followed by one of seven daughters. It is a curious fact that two such generations did follow each other after Sir Henry Tichborne had abolished the dole in 1796 and diverted the money to the Church. Whether from belief in the curse which thus seemed to be fulfilling itself, or from some other reason, the dole was restored and has never been interrupted since. It now takes the form of a ton and a half of flour from wheat grown on The Crawls. An open-air service is held on the steps of the church on Lady Day to which the public are admitted. The bin containing the flour is set before the church door; priest and congregation pray for the soul of Lady Mabella, and the flour is then blessed and distributed (89). Each man from Tichborne and Cheriton receives one gallon and half a gallon is given to every woman and child of the two villages.

The Biddenden Dole is usually said to be equally old and to have begun in 1100. There is, however, some doubt as to its actual date of origin, and it is probable that the custom was instituted much later. The founders were twin sisters, Eliza and Mary Chaulkhurst, who left twenty acres of land, still known as the Bread and Cheese Lands, in trust to the church-wardens of the parish to provide an annual dole of bread and cheese for the poor. Local tradition says that these women were joined together from birth by ligaments on the shoulders and hips. When they were thirty-four years old, one died, and the other was strongly urged by her friends to save herself by having the ligaments cut. She refused, saying that as they had come together so they would go, and six hours afterwards she also died. Hasted, the historian of Kent, says this story is without foundation, and probably arose from the two figures on the famous Biddenden cakes. The incident of the suggested

DOLES

operation is certainly extremely unlikely, for such a suggestion is not in accordance either with popular sentiment or surgical skill in the year 1100.

The distribution of bread and cheese now takes place on Easter Monday, and at the same time a thousand Biddenden cakes are given to all and sundry. These cakes are extremely hard and practically uneatable; they last for a long time and are more useful as souvenirs than as food. They are stamped with the figures of the two sisters standing side by side, with their names above their heads and the word "Biddenden" under their feet. On the apron of one is stamped 34, and on the other "in 1100," their age at the time of their death and the supposed date of its occurrence. Hasted says that originally the cakes were not stamped with figures or names, and that when the former were first introduced they were not intended to represent the sisters, but two poor widows, the most likely beneficiaries.

If the actual age of the Biddenden charity is uncertain, that of the Wayfarers' Dole at the Hospital of St. Cross is not. In one form or another it has been in existence for over eight hundred years. The Hospital was founded in 1133 by Henry de Blois as a shelter for thirteen poor men, and was later reformed by William de Wykeham after it had fallen on evil days through mismanagement. Cardinal Beaufort further extended it to include people of higher rank who had come to poverty through no fault of their own. The two charities still run side by side in this pleasant spot, the original poor men wearing black gowns and the others dark red. All wear the silver cross of the Knights Hospitallers of St. John, and each receives free accommodation, an allowance for food, and 5s. a week for pocket money. In Henry de Blois' time food was provided at the Hospital for a hundred poor people, and fifty years later the Bishop of Winchester increased the number to two hundred. To-day bread and ale are given without question to thirty-two people. The traveller knocks at the Porter's Lodge and is given his bread on an old carved platter and the ale in a horn bearing the arms of the Order. No conditions are laid down, and whoever asks may receive, though those who are really in want are given a larger portion.

A later wayfarers' charity was founded in 1579 by Richard

137

Watts of Rochester, who left money for "six poor travellers not being rogues or proctors" who were to receive a night's lodging, their food, and fourpence each. Those who seek his help to-day are given free shelter for the night, a supper of corned beef, bread and coffee, and 1s. 0½d. when they leave in the morning. At Ellington, near Huntingdon, a dole of bread is given in the church on Easter Monday. Only those who have slept in the parish overnight are eligible for the gift, and as this seems rather a curious condition to lay down for the un-travelled villagers of past centuries, it is possible that the charity was originally intended for poor travellers or pilgrims who might be passing through the parish at Eastertide.

In 1593 Lady Marvin bequeathed money to pay for 169 loaves for the poor of her district, and this charity is still carried on at Ufton Court, in Berkshire. As well as the bread, five yards of flannel and eleven yards of calico are given to nine poor people. The gifts are handed out to the recipients from a window at the back of the house on the Friday after the third Sunday in Lent.

At St. Briavels a basketful of bread and cheese is thrown to the people after the evening service on Whit Sunday. This custom is said to date from King John's time and to be a con-dition of tenure of certain lands given either by that King or by the Earl of Hereford to the village. The slices of bread and pieces of cheese are piled into a laundry basket and are thrown from the top of a high wall in a narrow lane. Men, women and children struggle for them as they fall, with a great deal of good-natured pushing and laughter until the last fragment has been thrown, after which the empty basket is held upside down for all to see, and the crowd disperses (90).

At Corfe Mullen, Thomas Phelips, who died in 1663, left money to provide ten poor people with twopennyworth of bread and twopennyworth of cheese every Sunday, a large amount in those days. The distribution was to be made at the base of the old cross in the churchyard, the cross itself having been thrown down by the Puritans some twenty years before. The bread and cheese have regularly been given every Sunday since Thomas Phelips died; until 1922 the distribution took place at the cross according to his wish, but it is now made less publicly, the food being taken round to the recipients' houses. In the same village in 1652 Richard Lockier founded a school for thirty scholars who were to receive free education, and to be catechised in the church every Whit Monday by the rector. This three-hundred-year-old custom is still kept up and the children, after the catechism, are presented with buns. Presumably to avoid all invidious distinctions, the rector is also given buns along with his flock. These little cakes also form part of the annual ceremony on the patronal festival of St. Bartholomew's Hospital at Sandwich. On the morning of August 24th a service is held and the name of the newly-chosen Master is announced. At noon the children arrive to run a race round the chapel, and afterwards each child is given a bun and fifty biscuits stamped with the arms of the Hospital are given to the grown-up people present.

At the Church of St. Bartholomew-the-Great in Smithfield, twenty-one sixpences are given to as many poor widows every Good Friday. The coins are placed on a tombstone in the churchyard (88), and each widow kneels by the stone to pick up her sixpence. She then walks over the stone and is given a hot cross bun and half a crown. No one now knows who gave the money for this charity, for all the papers concerning it perished with the other parish records in the Great Fire of London. The dole itself was in danger at one time, as the funds were diverted to other purposes, but a London antiquary generously came forward and arranged for the widows to receive their gifts as before.

This is not the only example of gifts connected with tombs or graves. At Leigh in Lancashire 5*s*. is presented on Maundy Thursday to forty poor people by the grave of Henry Travice who died in 1627. At Glentham in Lincolnshire seven old maids used to be given a shilling every Good Friday for washing a tomb with a figure on it known as Molly Grime. The water had to be brought from Newell Well. The history of this bequest seems to be lost and the custom itself died out about 1832. In 1611 Leonard Dare, of South Pool, Devonshire, arranged for threescore penny loaves to be given over his tombstone to the poor of the parish four times in every year. In Elizabeth's reign, Peter Symonds, a London merchant who must have loved children, left money to provide sixty new pennies and sixty packets of raisins to be given over his tomb on Good Friday to the youngest boys of the Blue Coat School, along with other more practical benefactions for the poor. These doles are still given every year but not over his grave, for that was obliterated when Liverpool Street Station was built.

This insistence on gifts being made by the tomb is curious and may be remotely connected with the primitive custom of sin-eating. In Wales and along the Welsh border, food was sometimes given over the coffin to some poor man who, by accepting it, was supposed to take upon himself the sins of the dead person. It is significant that the widows at St. Bartholomew's walk over the grave, and Peter Symonds' gifts were given formerly across his tombstone. Aubrey tells us that in Herefordshire in his time poor men, one of whom he seems to have seen, were given bread, beer and sixpence across the uncovered corpse on the bier, "in consideration whereof he (the sin-eater) tooke upon him (ipso facto) all the Sinnes of the Defunct, and freed him (or her) from walking after they were dead." Relics of this ancient custom lingered on in some country districts until quite recently. In Lancashire each funeral guest was given a bun and a slice of currant bread and a draught of spiced liquor before the coffin was closed. This was quite distinct from the funeral feast, which followed the burial. Mrs. Leather[1] tells us that only a few years before she wrote at the beginning of this century, a man at Hay was pressed to drink wine in the presence of a corpse, the reason given being that to do so would kill the sins of the dead woman. It may be that some confused notion of this sort lingered in the minds of those who founded these curious gravestone charities, and that those who accepted the gifts were, like the old sin-eaters, in some way supposed to bear away the sins of the giver.

Herrings are still distributed in Clavering in accordance with the will of John Thake, who in 1537 provided for a barrel of white herrings and a cade of red herrings to be given to the poor there during Lent. David Salter made a similar provision for the people of Farnham Royal and also left 2s. for a pair of kid gloves to be given to the clergyman on the first Sunday in Lent. Herrings seem to have been a favourite Lenten food, and at one time in Oxfordshire the children celebrated the end of Lent by going round in Holy Week singing

Herrings, herrings, white and red,
Ten a penny, Lent's dead.
Rise, dame, and give an egg
Or else a piece of bacon.
One for Peter, two for Paul,
Three for Jack-a-Lent's all
Away, Lent, away!

[1] E. M. Leather, *The Folklore of Herefordshire*.

If they did not receive what they wanted, they cut the latch or stopped up the keyhole with dirt as a sign of their displeasure.

At Sherfield-on-Loddon, Mr. Piggott Conant's Charity provides a Christmas dinner of beef and puddings for anyone in the parish who is too poor to buy such things for himself and who claims it as an indigent person. In the same county, at Ellingham, Dame Elizabeth Tipping, in 1687, ensured a happy Christmas for at least eight poor people by leaving the profits of land now known as the Poor's Allotment to be distributed amongst that number on St. Thomas' Day.

Alderman John Nash, of Worcester, who died in 1662, made a great many charitable bequests to the poor of his city, including the housing of "eight of the most impotent, decrepit, single men" and of two poor women appointed to look after them. He left directions that his will should be publicly read by the Town Clerk in the Guildhall on the first Friday in every Lent but, owing to the inordinate length of the document, the annual readings have been abandoned, and only at long intervals are the people of Worcester thus reminded of all he did for them.

Sexey's Hospital at Bruton is a lovely old building between the main street and the river, in which four married couples, five single men and seventeen single women, not being "drunkards, swearers, unquiet or disorderly persons" are housed. Their rooms are built round a quadrangle, and the upper ones have a charming balcony running in front of them. On one side are the dignified Visitors' rooms, the chapel and the hall, and behind the ground shelves steeply down to the river. Each inmate has his or her own plot of ground to cultivate, weekly pocket money, and a dress or a suit every three years. The Hospital was founded by Hugh Sexey, who was born in Bruton, or near it, and christened there on November 18th, 1556. He started life as a stable-boy at one of the inns, and Collinson tells us in his *History of Somerset* that "by the help of a little learning and by a regularity of meritorious conduct," he steadily advanced in the world. In spite of his poverty and apparent lack of influence, he rose to be one of the seven Auditors of the Exchequer, and died a very rich man. He never lost his interest in Bruton, and during his lifetime he conveyed certain lands to a body of Trustees to be used for charitable purposes.

Of these the chief was the Hospital, which was originally founded for eight poor people, but he evidently desired also to give other poor children a chance of that "learning" which had done so much for him. The Foundation's deed of incorporation calls for "the new building of a working house there for breeding of children and setting them to work, if it shall be so thought fit hereafter, and for raising money to bind children apprentices and after for stock for them." By way of beginning this "breeding of children," the Trustees elected twelve boys, who were to be clothed, maintained, and taught arithmetic, reading, and writing for three years, and afterwards to be apprenticed for seven years to mechanical trades, chiefly to carpenters and blacksmiths. The school was evidently run with careful economy. The Master was allowed 6s. or 7s. a week to board and clothe each child, and in 1839 an entry in the Minute Book records "That the Master be relieved from the expense of making shirts, of converting the boys' cloaks into breeches and trimming them, and of mending the boys' shoes."

This was the humble beginning of the two schools, one for boys and one for girls, which now exist at Bruton, and the mixed secondary school at Blackford. The first school and its system of apprenticeship were abolished in 1877, and now there are some six hundred children receiving education from the Foundation. This is a flowering which must be far beyond anything that Hugh Sexey ever dreamed, but it is certain that this progressive and kindly man would have approved it very heartily, had he ever envisaged the ambitious work now done in his name and with his money.

Many seventeenth-and eighteenth-century charities were founded for the improvement of learning and the encouragement of virtue which, in those days, usually meant simply diligence and obedience, at least as far as the poor were concerned. John Blagrave, the Reading mathematician and connoisseur of sundials, who died in 1611, left twenty nobles to be competed for annually by three maidservants who could prove they were of good character and had served for five years in one household. This money is still paid; the girls who are qualified to compete go to Reading Town Hall on Good Friday and there cast lots for the prize before the Mayor and Aldermen. There is a somewhat similar charity in London but here the gambling element is missing. In 1620, Isaac

89 The Tichborne dole: Sir Anthony Tichborne hands out the flour to the villagers

90 The end of the Whit Sunday bread and cheese distribution at St. Briavel's, Gloucestershire

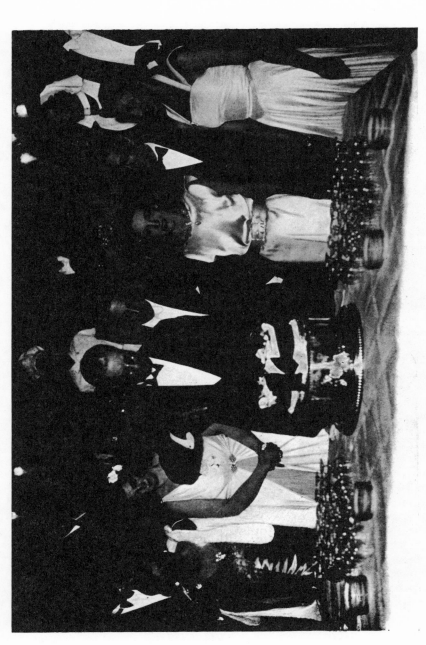

91   Cutting the Baddeley Cake at Drury Lane for the 144th time, by Mr. C. M. Lowne, trustee of the fund, in the presence of the Company playing

Duckett left a house and lands in Crayford, the rents of which were to provide wedding portions for four maidservants, two from St. Clement Danes parish and two from that of St. Andrew's, Holborn. The girls had to provide certificates showing five years' good service in one house, and this is still the qualification. The lands have greatly increased in value since Isaac Duckett's day, and the Trustees are now able to provide money gifts for many more than the four brides mentioned in the will.

Testators often left money to pay for an annual sermon to inculcate some special lesson or to commemorate some important event. In 1795 Richard Johnson provided for a sermon in Hendon Parish Church on the depressing text, "Human Life is but a bubble," and this is still preached every year before the members of the Stationers' Company who afterwards inspect his grave in the churchyard. Another sermon connected with a grave is that arranged for by Mary Gibson in 1773. It is given on August 12th, and a condition of the bequest is that the Governors of Christ's Hospital shall annually inspect her tomb at Sutton in Surrey and satisfy themselves that it is in good order and has not been disturbed. This was a precaution against the body-snatchers whose activities in the eighteenth and early nineteenth centuries were greatly feared, and with good reason.

The famous Lion Sermon has been preached every October 16th in the Church of St. Katharine Cree for three hundred years. It commemorates Sir John Gayer's escape from lions during one of his trading expeditions. Becoming separated from his companions, he suddenly found himself confronted by lions and, in his extremity, said the prayer of Daniel. The lions turned away, leaving him unharmed, and he lived to be twice Lord Mayor of London, in 1646 and 1647, and to suffer imprisonment for his devotion to Charles I and his refusal to subsidise Parliamentary troops from the City of London funds. He lived in stormy times and must have been through many dangers in the course of his expeditions as a Merchant Adventurer, but it was his escape from the lions that most deeply impressed him and caused him to leave money to provide for a sermon to be preached every year on the anniversary of his deliverance.

A more curious sermon bequest is found at Berrow, Worcestershire, where Mrs. Susannah Cocks Nanfan left £2 yearly from the proceeds of a field called the Bloody Meadow, to be paid to the Vicar of Berrow for preaching an annual sermon against duelling.

The distribution of Pax Cakes at Hentland is supposed to have been founded in 1570 by Lady Scudamore, who charged the revenues of Baysham Court with an annual sum to pay for cake and beer on Palm Sunday for the parishioners of Hentland, Sellack, and King's Capel. Her object in doing so was to promote a spirit of peace and good fellowship amongst them by the institution of a common meal in which all could partake in amity. She selected Palm Sunday as the most suitable date, so that all might be at peace with their neighbours before they made their Easter Communion. Originally one large cake was made. It was presented by the churchwardens to the vicar, who cut the first slice; the remainder was then taken round to each person in the congregation and was eaten in church. Glasses of beer were also handed round, but this part of the ceremony has long been obsolete and the money set aside to pay for the beer has been lost. At the present time small cakes are made with the impress of the Paschal lamb and flag upon them. They are handed to the parishioners as they leave the church, and with each one the old greeting of "God and Good Neighbourhood" is given by the priest.

At Kidderminster also peace between neighbours is annually promoted, in this case by a dinner on Midsummer Eve. A maiden lady whose name has been lost bequeathed the sum of forty shillings about five hundred years ago to provide farthing loaves for every child born or living in Church Street. She also expressed a wish that all the men of the street should meet once a year and settle any differences which might have arisen between them during the previous twelve months. In 1778 John Brecknell, himself an inhabitant of Church Street, left a sum of £150 "for the better establishment and continuance of the said friendly meeting for ever." Every child and unmarried person in the street was to receive a twopenny plum cake in addition to the loaf already given and pipes, tobacco, and ale were to be provided for the men who attended the Midsummer Eve assembly. Any money left over was to be distributed to the poor in sums of not less than two or more than five shillings for each person.

To-day the celebration takes the form of the famous Peace and Good Neighbourhood Dinner, which the chairman opens by asking whether anyone in Church Street is at odds with his neighbour and offering to try and compose the difference, if any such exists. "Peace and Good Neighbourhood" is the principal toast at the dinner, and these words are said when the cakes and loaves, and the money gifts to the poor, are taken round to the houses. This desire for unity seems always to have been strong in Kidderminster. It was here that Richard Baxter, the nonconformist minister, lived and worked from 1641 to 1660. He was a man with ideas far in advance of his time, and throughout his stay he strove for religious tolerance and the absence of strife. On his memorial in the centre of the town, which churchmen and nonconformists united to raise in 1875, appear these words:

In a stormy and divided age
he advocated unity and comprehension
Pointing the way to
The Everlasting Rest.

As a sign that at least a part of this lesson was learnt by his fellow-townsmen, his pulpit is now kept in his chapel and his chair in the parish church.

A pleasant little ceremony of friendship and conviviality is held every year in the Green Room of Drury Lane Theatre in honour of Baddeley, the chef who became an actor. He is said to have cooked a particularly excellent dinner for Foote, the distinguished actor, and the latter offered him anything he wanted as a reward. He asked for a part in one of the theatre productions; it was granted to him and he became quite successful in his new profession. When he died in 1794, he left £100 for a cake to be made and cut in his memory every year on Twelfth Night after the end of the performance (91). It is known as the Baddeley Cake, and is brought in by the attendants of the theatre in their eighteenth-century liveries and powdered wigs. Baddeley also had the right to wear a livery in his lifetime, for the actor-members of Drury Lane were allowed to wear Royal livery and to style themselves "His Majesty's Servants." This is a privilege they still enjoy, though no one now avails himself of it; Baddeley himself is said to have been one of the last members of the company to do so.

Those who do not wish to leave money to charity can usually find excellent reasons for not doing so, but few put them on record in their wills. One man, however, who died in 1687, took the opportunity of stating his clear views on the whole subject of charitable bequests and gifts, though as will be seen, he had not entirely the courage of his convictions. This was Sir William Petty, the inventor and economist, who seems to have enjoyed the best of both worlds politically while he lived. He was secretary to the Lord Lieutenant of Ireland during the Protectorate and a Member of Parliament under Richard Cromwell, and was knighted by Charles II after the Restoration. In his will he says:

"As for legacies to the poor, I am at a stand; as for beggars by trade and election, I give them nothing; as for impotents by the hand of God, the public ought to maintain them; as for those who have no calling or estate, they should be put upon their kindred; as for those who can get no work, the magistrates should cause them to be employed, which may well be done in Ireland, where is fifteen acres of improvable land for every head; prisoners for crimes by the king; for debts, by their prosecutors; as for those who compassionate the sufferings of any object, let them relieve themselves by relieving such sufferers—that is, give them alms *pro re nata*, and for God's sake relieve the several species above mentioned, if the above-mentioned obligees fail in their duty. Wherefore, I am contented that I have assisted all my poor relations, and put many in the way of getting their own bread, and have laboured in public works, and by inventions have sought out real objects of charity; I do hereby conjure all who partake of my estate, from time to time, to do the same at their peril. Nevertheless, to answer custom, and to take the surer side, I give £20 to the most wanting of the parish, in which I may die."

BIBLIOGRAPHY

ADDY, S. O.	Household Tales and Traditional Remains
AUBREY, J.	Remaines of Gentilisme and Judaisme
ANDREWS, W.	Bygone Derbyshire
BARRETT, C. R. B.	Essex, Highways, Byways and Waterways (2 Series)
BEDDINGTON, W., AND CHRISTY, E.	It Happened in Hampshire
BOYD, A. W.	The Comberbach (Cheshire) Version of the Soul-Caking Play
BRAND, J.	Observations on the Popular Antiquities of Great Britain
BRYANT, A.	Charles II
BURROWS, M.	Worthies of All Souls
CHAMBERS, R.	The Book of Days
CHAMBERS, R. W.	England Before the Norman Conquest
COURTENAY, M. A.	Cornish Feasts and Folklore
DACOMBE, M. R.	Dorset Up Along and Down Along
DITCHFIELD, P. H.	Old English Customs
FOLKARD, R.	Plant Lore, Legends and Lyrics
FRAZER, SIR J. G.	The Golden Bough
GOMME, G. L.	Ethnology in Folklore
	The Village Community
HARDWICK, C.	History of the Borough of Preston
	Traditions, Superstitions and Folklore
HARLAND, J., AND WILKINSON, T.	Lancashire Folklore
HEANLEY, R. M.	The Vikings: Their Folklore in Marshland (Saga Book of the Viking Club)
HENDERSON, W.	Folklore of the Northern Counties
HOLE, C.	English Folklore
	Traditions and Customs of Cheshire
HOPE, R. S.	Holy Wells
HULL, E.	Folklore of the British Isles
LEATHER, E. M.	The Folklore of Herefordshire
LONG, G.	The Folklore Calendar
MAGRATH, J. R.	The Queen's College
MUNCEY, R. W.	Our Old English Fairs
MURRAY, M.	The God of the Witches
OLIVIER, E.	Moonrakings

PESHALL, SIR J.	The Antient and Present State of Oxford
PLOT, DR.	Natural History of Staffordshire
RICE-OXLEY, L.	Oxford Renowned
SEDDON, W. H.	Painswick Feast
SMITH, W. G.	Dunstable
STEWART-BROWN, E.	The Chester Hand or Glove (Chester Archeological Society's Journal)
STOW, J.	Survey of London
TIDDY, R. J.	The Mummers' Play
URLIN, E.	Festivals, Holy Days and Saints' Days
WALFORD, C.	Fairs, Past and Present
WILLIAMS, IOLO	English Folk Song and Dance
COUNTY FOLKLORE	Gloucestershire, ed. E. S. Hartland
	Leicestershire and Rutlandshire, ed. C. J. Billson
	Suffolk, ed. Lady C. E. Gurdon

Notes and Queries
The Cheshire Sheaf
The Gentleman's Magazine
Transactions of the Devonshire Association
Transactions of the Lancashire and Cheshire Antiquarian Society

INDEX

The illustrations are referred to in heavier type under their figure numbers.

149